CW01084121

STAR CARR:
Life in Britain
after the Ice Age

Archaeology for All
Council for British Archaeology

STAR CARR:
Life in Britain after the Ice Age

Nicky Milner
Barry Taylor
Chantal Conneller
Tim Schadla-Hall

Archaeology for All
Council for British Archaeology 2013

Published in 2013 by the Council for British Archaeology
St Mary's House, 66 Bootham, York, YO30 7BZ

Copyright © 2013 Authors and Council for British Archaeology

British Library cataloguing in Publication Data
A catalogue record for this book is available from the British Library
ISBN 978-1-902771-99-1

DOI 10.11141/AfA1

Typeset by Carnegie Book Production
Printed and bound by Lavenham Press Ltd

Cover image: Artist's reconstruction of the site at Star Carr (Dominic Andrews)

We dedicate this book to John Moore, without whom we might never have known anything about the site of Star Carr.

We also dedicate it to Richard Marriott, Richard Senior and Graham Harvey, the local contingent of the Vale of Pickering Research Trust who for over 25 years have provided generous support as fundraisers and treasurer. Without their support, we would never have found many of the other sites, and we would not have been able to map the contours of the ancient lake.

Contents

List of Figures

Around 11,000 years ago, several hundred years after the end of the last Ice Age, groups of humans began to settle around the shores of a large lake that had formed across the eastern end of the Vale of Pickering, in what is now North Yorkshire. The area that they inhabited was very different from anything that we would recognise today, with birch woodland covering much of the landscape. Dense beds of reeds and other wetland plants were growing around the edge of the lake and communities of aquatic plants thrived in the deeper waters further from the shore. Wild animals, such as deer, elk and bear, roamed the forest, fish swam in the lake, and birds flitted amongst the trees and through the reeds. Today, this landscape has been replaced by one of roads, fields, farms and houses. Cows and sheep graze across land where elk and bear once lived, and farmers drive tractors where hunters once stalked their prey. Even the lake has disappeared, gradually filling in with sediments over thousands of years. But the remains of this landscape, and the traces of the people who originally inhabited it, have been preserved, buried beneath thick deposits of peat that have formed across this area. This book tells the story of these people, and in particular the lives of those who settled at one of the most important archaeological sites in Britain: Star Carr.

The importance of Star Carr

The site known as Star Carr was first discovered in 1948 and after several years of excavation became world-famous in archaeological circles. It belongs to a period known as the Mesolithic (or Middle

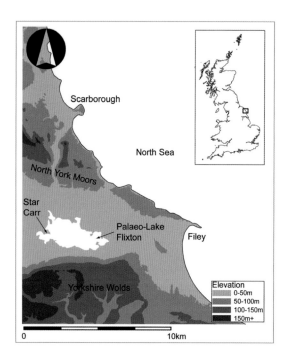

Figure 1.1 *The location of Lake Flixton in the Vale of Pickering*

Stone Age), a time before farming, when people lived by hunting animals and gathering plants for food. We refer to people who live in this way as 'hunter-gatherers', and it is a way of life that has characterised much of our human past. The wonderful collection of artefacts recovered during the excavations has made Star Carr the most iconic site of this period and it is sometimes referred to as the 'Stonehenge of the Mesolithic' because of its importance.

The Mesolithic period occurred long before the introduction and use of metal and pottery, so the main archaeological finds are usually stone (flint) tools and the flakes of flint waste created when making the tools. However, other materials were used at this time: people ate a wide range of different foods, and made things out of animal products such as bone, sinews, antler and hides, as well as out of wood and other plant materials. The problem with such materials is that they are organic and thus easily rot, so they tend not to be found on most archaeological sites.

Star Carr, however, is different: at this site, bone, antler and wood have all been found. These normally perishable remains have been preserved for thousands of years because they were deposited in waterlogged peat, which has the properties necessary to prevent decay. We therefore have a rare insight into aspects of Mesolithic life which have usually long since disappeared and this is what is so exciting about Star Carr: it tells a story of the Mesolithic past that no other site has been able to do.

The rare artefacts that have been discovered at the site include 'frontlets' or head-dresses made of red deer skulls, beautifully crafted barbed points made out of red deer antler used for hunting and fishing, and beads made of amber and shale. Recent excavations at the site have also discovered wooden timbers that had been worked using axes – these represent the earliest evidence of carpentry in Europe. Since its initial discovery in 1948, there have been many attempts to find another Mesolithic site like Star Carr, but although sites with organic remains have been found, rather frustratingly none has produced the same types, numbers and range of artefacts.

The site has also developed an air of mystery: there have been many different interpretations about how it may have been used and occupied, which vary from a hunting camp where people congregated to hunt animals such as red deer, to a base camp where families were living at certain times of the year, or a site where ritual activities took place. Numerous articles have been written about it, but there is still a general feeling that we don't really understand what was going on there. This was even highlighted in a recent edition of the magazine *British Archaeology*: one of the '10 big questions archaeology must answer' was 'What was Star Carr?'.

Our recent work at the site has resulted in a whole new set of exciting findings, which have inevitably raised a new set of questions to be answered. The discovery of what turned out to be a 'house', dubbed by the press as the 'earliest house in Britain', resulted in the site being recognised nationally and consequently it was scheduled in 2011 as a monument of national importance by the Department for Culture, Media and Sport. The Minister, John Penrose, said: 'The diversity of finds on offer at Star Carr and its history which goes back to 9000 BC are unequalled in British archaeology and it remains one of the most important Mesolithic sites in Europe'.

Figure 1.2
Mesolithic worked flint

What does 'Star Carr' mean?

Star Carr was the name of both the field to the north of the Hertford Cut (a canalised river) and the farm which owned the site when it was first excavated. People often ask what Star Carr actually means; according to Peter Rowley-Conwy it is thought to have Danish origins. This area of North Yorkshire was settled by the Vikings and was part of the Danelaw. 'Star Carr' is thought to come from the Danish words *star kjær* which simply mean sedge fen. Sedge is one of the main grass-like plants which would have been growing in the wetlands and fen is a name for a type of wetland environment.

Figure 1.3 *A sedge fen of the type that Star Carr was named after*

The importance of peat

However, Star Carr is only one part of the story, and in more recent years archaeologists have been attempting to understand the site within its wider landscape context. This is no easy task because the landscape has changed so dramatically in the 11,000 years since Star Carr was occupied. Today, looking north from the village of Flixton, there are green fields with animals grazing and you could be forgiven for thinking that there had never been a lake here. However, if you were to walk out onto the fields you would find that the soil is very dark brown in colour and in some places boggy; if someone were to jump up and down on it you would feel the ground wobbling slightly – this is because you are walking over peat.

This blanket of peat hides a Mesolithic landscape which has been slowly mapped out through years of survey and excavation. We now have a good idea of where the edges of Lake Flixton were and from this have been able to dig trenches to find other Mesolithic sites. In addition, the peat has enabled pollen and the remains of plants and insects to survive; this allows us to reconstruct the environment and how it changed through time.

Unfortunately, due to changing land use and drainage, large areas of the peat are drying out which has a negative impact on the archaeology: much of the bone and antler has decayed or has been completely destroyed in the last 50 years, and the wood is also in bad condition. Nevertheless, recent excavations have shown there is still much to learn from Star Carr and the other sites in this landscape and further research is necessary in order to learn more about this hidden, past world before it is lost forever.

The Mesolithic and Star Carr

This book aims to tell the story of Star Carr and its landscape, as we currently understand it. Before describing the discovery of Star Carr itself, we start with an overview of the Mesolithic period which sets out a framework of dates and terms and explains the key concepts relating to how people would have lived at that time. The Mesolithic is a fascinating time period which starts with abrupt climate change and incorporates a range of environmental events. People living at this time would have had very different lives from ours, and yet there are many fascinating resonances for us: they built houses, they made beads, and they had domesticated dogs.

In Chapter 3 we move on to the history of research at Star Carr from the initial discovery of the site by a local amateur archaeologist, John Moore, and the subsequent excavations by Grahame Clark of the University of Cambridge, and then two investigations by the Vale of Pickering Research Trust. The discoveries and artefacts are described and we explain the various interpretations that have been made. We then explore the wider context of the lake in Chapter 4: how we have discovered where its margins are and how other sites have been found and excavated. We also explain how we can reconstruct the environment and climate during the Mesolithic from the environmental records that are locked in the peat. Finally, we use all the evidence to paint a picture of life at Star Carr and attempt to explain how people might have lived 11,000 years ago.

Figure 1.4 *(overleaf) The Vale of Pickering as it looks today*

What is peat?

Peat is a deposit made up of partially decomposed plant material, which forms in wet environments such as lakes and marshes. When plants growing in these environments die, the wet conditions can slow down the rate at which their remains decay. As more plant material builds up, the lower part of the deposit can become compressed, preventing oxygen from reaching it. This slows down the decay process even further and creates an environment where organic materials, such as plant remains, and objects made from bone, wood, or antler, can survive for thousands of years.

The build-up of these deposits was also responsible for the eventual disappearance of Lake Flixton and the formation of the peat-covered landscape we see today. Shortly after the start of the Mesolithic, peat began to form around the lake shore. As these deposits became thicker, they caused the water around the edge of the lake to become shallower, and wetland plants and even trees began to grow directly on the peat. Over time, the lake became smaller and shallower until, by the end of the Mesolithic, there was just a series of small shallow pools surrounded by marshes and fens.

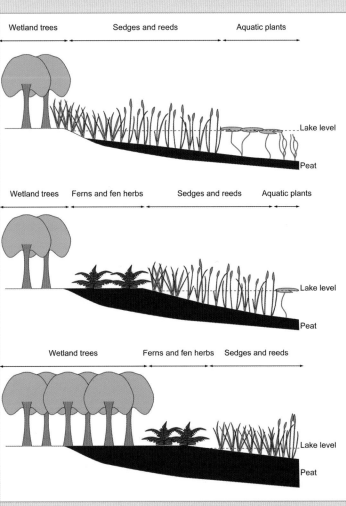

Figure 1.5 *(top) Layers of peat that formed at the edge of the lake, recorded during archaeological excavations at Flixton School House Farm in 2008*

Figure 1.6 *Diagram showing the development of the lake-edge environments during the early Mesolithic*

The Mesolithic

2

Introduction

The Mesolithic is an exciting period to study because there is so much to discover: compared with other periods, it has largely been ignored by academics and archaeologists, and so with every site that is excavated new perspectives are gained. It has perhaps been overlooked because it has been viewed as sitting between what are sometimes considered to be two more exciting periods: the Palaeolithic with its remarkable cave art, and the Neolithic with its impressive and enigmatic monuments, as well as the beginnings of farming and the first polished stone tools and pottery.

The period is significant for several reasons. The first is that it starts at the end of the last Ice Age with a period of rapid climate change. One of the big questions for Mesolithic researchers is how did people adapt to the significant climate and environmental changes between about 10,000 and 9000 BC. Other interesting natural events within the Mesolithic include a tsunami in the North Sea and the breaching of the Strait of Dover which resulted in Britain becoming an island. People at this time were practical and able to live in a range of different landscapes because they made tools out of natural resources and found food from a variety of places in the landscape. Through an examination of the finds from Mesolithic sites, we can begin to reconstruct what life must have been like for people at this time.

We can also use ethnographic evidence to explain how hunter-gatherers lived, that is by studying people who still live by hunting and gathering today. Perhaps some of the best data for comparison with Europe come from peoples in the Arctic Circle and Siberia, who appear to have many similarities with Mesolithic people. Although present-day hunter-gatherers have inevitably been influenced by the modern world, they do still maintain many ancient traditions and customs which can help archaeologists understand a world far removed from their own, and encourage them to view the evidence with which they are presented with an open mind.

This chapter first sets the scene and explains how we define the Mesolithic and when it was. We also look at how the climate changed and how this impacted on the natural environment. We then explore the technology of the period and how people used natural resources in the environment to make things. Stone tools were essential to survival in this period because people relied on them for the majority of their day-to-day activities, but other materials taken from animals and plants were incredibly important too and help to paint a broader picture. Finally,

Early definitions of terms

The 'Palaeolithic' and 'Neolithic' periods were defined by Sir John Lubbock in 1865:

I. That of the Drift: when man shared the possession of Europe with the Mammoth, the Cave Bear, the Woolly-haired rhinoceros, and other extinct animals. This we may call the 'Paleolithic' period.

II. The later or Polished Stone Age; a period characterised by beautiful weapons and instruments made of flint and other kinds of stone; in which, however, we find no trace of the knowledge of any metal … This we may call the 'Neolithic' period.

The term 'Mesolithic' was initially coined by Hodder Westropp in 1872 in order to define three phases of using stone tools:

1. The flint implements of the gravel drift, and of the cave period, evidently used by man in his lowest and most barbarous grade. [Palaeolithic]

2. The flint implements (the flint flakes, and the chipped flints) found on the surface in England, Ireland, Denmark, and other countries, which belonged to a people who lived by the chase. [Mesolithic]

3. Ground and polished stone implements which mark a more advanced stage, and which are associated with traces of a pastoral age. [Neolithic]

John Evans' book, *Ancient Stone Implements*, also published in 1872, was much more detailed, but continued to use only the terms Palaeolithic and Neolithic. It has been suggested that because there was so much uncertainty about what the term 'Mesolithic' represented and where it fitted into the Stone Age sequence it was not used again until the 1900s.

we consider human behaviour. People in the Mesolithic were physically very similar to people today but their ways of living would have been very different. We use the evidence we have so far to build up a picture of how people lived their lives between about 9600 and 4000 BC.

Setting the scene

What is the Mesolithic?

Mesolithic means middle Stone Age (meso = middle, lithic = stone), and it sits between the Palaeolithic (old Stone Age) and Neolithic (new Stone Age). Unlike some later periods such as the Roman or Viking eras, which are loosely defined by the influx of a group of people, the Mesolithic is a much more arbitrary definition.

Miles Burkitt, the first-ever lecturer in Prehistory at Cambridge University, wrote a text book in 1926 on *Our Early Ancestors. An Introductory study of Mesolithic, Neolithic and Copper Age Cultures in Europe and Adjacent regions.* At the start of this, he explains that the older prehistorians did not admit the Mesolithic period as a separate entity. He goes on to say that the Palaeolithic and Neolithic were distinguished by whether or not they (1) had pottery, (2) had domestic animals and agriculture, and (3) whether polishing/ grinding were used in making stone tools, or simply chipping. He defines the end of the Palaeolithic/start of the Mesolithic as a period when there was a rapid change of temperature and the climate improved, and the end of the Mesolithic as the time of the introduction of polished stone axes and megalithic tombs. This broad definition is still used today.

Grahame Clark became a PhD student of Miles Burkitt in the 1920s and from his analysis of Mesolithic flint industries in Britain went on to become the leading expert in Mesolithic research until his death in 1995.

Figure 2.1 *Sir Grahame Clark*

How we date sites

Before radiocarbon dating was developed, archaeologists had to rely on other methods to understand the chronology of the past. The most fundamental of these methods (and one that we still use today) is stratigraphy. This is the idea that if layers of sediment build up over time, the layers on the bottom will be older than those on the top. If these layers contain archaeological material, such as flint tools or other artefacts, then it follows that those in the lower layers will be older than those higher up. We refer to this as a 'relative chronology', as the artefacts are placed in date order, relative to one another.

Another form of relative dating is known as 'typology'. This involves classifying artefacts such as flint tools into 'types' or styles, based on their form and the technology used to produce them. By establishing which of these 'types' are older than others, archaeologists are able to date sites based on the sorts of artefacts that they found there. In the 19th century it was thought that artefact typology developed in a similar way to biological evolution, with the older types being more primitive or simple than the newer ones. Although we no longer think that this is true, we still use the presence of certain types of artefacts to identify sites of particular periods.

In the early 20th century, archaeologists working in Scandinavia developed a more accurate method of dating using the relatively new science of pollen analysis. During the previous decades, botanists had used pollen preserved in lakes and peat bogs to establish a record of the plant communities that had formed in Northern Europe since the last Ice Age. By looking at the pollen from sediments that contained archaeological material, it became possible to relate the site to a particular period in Europe's environmental history. Although this did not provide a precise date, it did allow archaeologists to determine whether different sites were earlier, later, or broadly contemporary with one another without having to rely on the less reliable methods of typology. In the 1930s the botanists Harry and Mary Godwin used this technique to show that antler artefacts found in peat bogs in Yorkshire were broadly contemporary with the Mesolithic sites that had been excavated in Scandinavia. This provided the first conclusive evidence that artefacts in Britain formed part of a much wider Mesolithic tradition that extended across Northern Europe.

Radiocarbon dating, however, has revolutionised the way in which archaeologists understand the past, by providing the potential for calendar date ranges. In 1949 (the same year as Clark started working at Star Carr), Willard Libby, a Professor of Chemistry at the University of Chicago, published the first radiocarbon dates following several years of secret research. In 1960 he was awarded the Nobel Prize for Chemistry for his work on radiocarbon dating.

Carbon is a component of all organic compounds. It exists in nature as three different isotopes: ^{12}C, ^{13}C and ^{14}C. Radioactive carbon (^{14}C) is unstable and decays at a constant rate. It is produced in the atmosphere and absorbed by plants which are then eaten by animals and humans and incorporated into their skeletons. This uptake of radiocarbon stops when the plant or animal dies. Libby recognised that because radiocarbon decays through time it is possible to measure the amount left in a sample to give the date of death. Laboratories can measure the atoms of ^{14}C to produce radiocarbon dates and these will be reported with a range of + or − so many years. Radiocarbon dates are reported in bp, which stands for 'Before Present', and radiocarbon laboratories all use AD 1950 as a standard 'present' date. However, because the concentration of ^{14}C in the atmosphere has not been constant through time we have to adjust the dates to take account of this variation. This adjustment has been achieved by dating tree rings of known age and producing a calibration curve which laboratories use to calibrate the radiocarbon dates accordingly and convert the bp date into a BC or AD date.

So, for instance, at Star Carr, a date on an antler splinter produced a date of 9670 +/- 100 bp. The date was then calibrated using the calibration curve to 9300–8700 BC at a 95.4% probability, meaning that there is a 95.4% chance that the true date of that sample falls within the given date range.

Figure 2.2 *The last 12,000 years of the human past*

2,000 AD	Medieval & Modern Periods	• Development of the internet
		• Shakespeare's plays are first performed
1,000 AD	Saxon England & the Celtic Kingdoms	• The Battle of Hastings
		• The first written law codes, histories and literature
	Roman Britain	• Hadrian's Wall is built
0		• The first coins are minted
	The Iron Age	
1,000 BC		• Development of iron working
	The Bronze Age	• The Dover Boat set sail
2,000 BC		• Building of the trilathons at Stonehenge
		• Development of bronze working
3,000 BC	The Neolithic	• First phase of construction at Stonehenge
4,000 BC		• Earliest evidence for domestic crops and animals
5,000 BC		• The Severn Estuary footprints
6,000 BC		• Britain becomes an island
7,000 BC	The Mesolithic	
8,000 BC		• The Howick house is built
9,000 BC		• Star Carr is first occupied
		• End of the Ice Age
10,000 BC		

Since these early beginnings almost a century ago, archaeology has seen the development of radiocarbon dating which has enabled us to define the beginning and end of the period more closely. The beginning is generally taken to be the end of the last Ice Age and the period of rapid warming at the start of the current geological epoch, the Holocene, at about 9600 BC.

The end of the Mesolithic, or beginning of the Neolithic, is thought to occur at about 4000 BC in Britain. However, there is much debate about when the Neolithic starts, and what we mean by the Neolithic. As we have seen, the Neolithic was first defined by the occurrence of polished stone tools but nowadays we see it representing the introduction of a whole range of new things including pottery, monumental tombs (such as the West Kennet long barrow) and the introduction of farming, which includes domesticated animals and grains. However, each of these things may have been introduced into different parts of Britain at slightly different times. Therefore, some people would put the start of the Neolithic several centuries before 4000 BC, based on evidence of incoming pottery; others might put it several centuries after 4000 BC based on dates from the monumental tombs. It is probably safest to talk in terms of a 'transition' in the centuries around 4000 BC and not to assume that all new products and ideas arrived in Britain at the same time.

However much we debate the exact beginning and end of the Mesolithic, the key point is that the Mesolithic covers a huge span of time lasting about 5600 years. So, if we look at a timeline from the present day back 11,600 years to the end of the Ice Age, the Mesolithic encompasses almost half of that time!

Textbooks have tended to conflate these 5600 years and talk about the Mesolithic as if nothing much changed within that period. This is probably because we know relatively little about what happened, and only recently have we begun to think about how life may have changed for people over this lengthy period of time. In Britain we divide the Mesolithic into two main parts, the Early and the Late Mesolithic, based on changes in flint technology, the division occurring at some point around 8000 BC. In other parts of Europe the Mesolithic has been split up in different ways. In Denmark the era is divided into the Early, Middle and Late Mesolithic, the Danish Early Mesolithic being known as the Maglemosian, a name taken from the site of Maglemose in Denmark. This term is sometimes used when referring to Early Mesolithic sites in Northern Europe which have similar technologies: for instance, Star Carr is sometimes referred to as a Maglemosian site.

Climate change

Today, Britain is an island with a temperate climate; it is separated from the continental mainland by the English Channel and the North Sea. Over the past million years, however, the climate has oscillated between periods of extreme cold (known as glacial stages) and warmer temperatures (known as interglacial stages) that have transformed the landscape of Britain and Europe. The last of these cold (glacial) stages began about 80,000 years ago and reached its height 22,000 years ago when much of Britain and Northern Europe was covered with massive glaciers. Over the next few thousand years the climate warmed slightly, causing the glaciers to retreat, and allowing species of arctic plants and animals (including reindeer) to begin to colonise the landscape. This was a harsh and inhospitable environment, however, and humans appear to have avoided settling in Britain at this time. Sea levels were much lower and much of what is now the southern part of the North Sea would have been dry ground, connecting Britain to continental Europe.

Then, around 12,700 BC there was a relatively rapid warming of the Earth's climate, with summer temperatures in Britain rising to around 20°C. As plant species responded to the warmer climate the British landscape was gradually transformed as grassland, scrub, and eventually birch woodland became established. Animals such as elk, red deer, horse and brown bear crossed the North Sea plain and eventually human communities began to recolonise Britain: evidence for people is found at a number of sites, including Creswell Crags in Derbyshire.

At around 10,900 BC the climate suddenly deteriorated again, possibly as a result of the melting of the North American ice sheets, which caused a massive influx of fresh water from a previously ice-dammed lake into the ocean. This would have disrupted the North Atlantic Ocean currents which circulate warm waters from the tropics northwards. Summer temperatures in Britain would have fallen significantly and the winters became long and harsh, with temperatures as low as -10°C. Glaciers began to re-form in the Highlands of Scotland and the uplands of England and Wales, whilst the remainder of the country was transformed into an open desolate landscape of grassland and scrub as the cold temperatures and short growing season limited the growth of trees and many other species of plants. This cold phase is known as the Younger Dryas, named after an alpine-tundra wildflower, *Dryas octopetala*, and it marks the very end of the last Ice Age.

There is much debate about whether people remained in Britain during the Younger Dryas. We know that species of animals that were suited to cold environments, such as reindeer, arctic hare, and horse, continued to inhabit this area and could have been a source of food for any surviving human groups. However, archaeological evidence for human occupation around this time is very sparse and the radiocarbon dates we have are not precise enough to tell whether these sites are contemporary with the Younger Dryas or are slightly later. At the moment there is no evidence to say conclusively that humans were present in Britain but it remains a gripping question and one that future research may well resolve.

The Younger Dryas ended extremely abruptly at some point around 9600 BC with another period of rapid climate change. In Britain, summer temperatures rose by as much as 10°C in a matter of decades and plants suited to temperate environments became established once more. To begin with, these comprised mostly grasses, herbaceous plants and scrub vegetation, such as willow, but within 300 years large areas of birch woodland had grown up across much of the country. We refer to the period of open grassland environments as the Preboreal and the subsequent phase of woodland as the Boreal. Although the climate had warmed, it was by no means stable, and the period following the end of the Younger Dryas witnessed a series of climatic fluctuations. The earliest, and perhaps most severe, occurred between approximately 9400 and 9200 BC and is known as the Preboreal Oscillation.

The rapid warming of the climate and the changing patterns of vegetation also had a dramatic effect on the animal populations. As temperatures rose, arctic species such as reindeer died out and were replaced by temperate species, such as elk, deer, and wild boar, which crossed into Britain over the North Sea Plain. Then, as the woodlands developed, horse also became locally extinct, and remained absent from Britain until it was reintroduced in the Bronze Age, over 7000 years later. We are less sure about when humans were present in Britain following the rapid climate change. The earliest radiocarbon dates for Mesolithic activity come from Star Carr, and indicate that the site was inhabited from around 9000 BC. However, it is likely that humans were also present in the centuries before this, inhabiting the open grassland of the Preboreal landscape.

The effects of sea-level rise

The rapid climate change at the beginning of the Preboreal meant significant rises in sea level as the warmer climate resulted in the melting of ice sheets, causing changes to the coastline around Britain. During the Early Mesolithic, Britain was still a peninsula linked to the rest of Europe by a landmass in the North Sea known as Doggerland. This was a rich, low-lying landscape, dissected by rivers and dotted with lakes and wetlands. We know this was a place in which Mesolithic people lived due to finds that have been dredged up from the bottom of the sea in the nets of trawlers. Amongst the material recovered from the area are tools made from stone, bone and antler, animal bones and human remains.

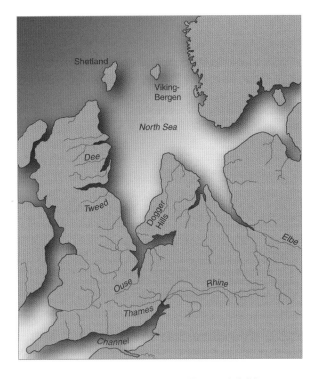

Figure 2.3 *Map showing the extent of 'Doggerland', the North Sea Plain that connected Britain to the continental mainland during the early Mesolithic*

Doggerland existed until sometime between 6500 and 6200 BC, when it was finally flooded by rising sea levels. Dogger Island, the area of the present Dogger Bank, may have persisted until around 5000 BC before becoming submerged.

At about the same time, c 6200 BC, a tsunami occurred in the North Sea. This was caused by an underwater landslide off the coast of Norway known as the Storegga Slide, involving an area of about 20,000 km². The study of sediments has demonstrated that a large tidal wave would have hit various parts of the coastlines of Norway, Scotland and Northern England, and no doubt would have had a terrible impact on Mesolithic coastal communities living there at the time. It has even been argued that it led to the final abandonment of Dogger Island.

Rising sea levels would have inundated ancestral territories, submerged woodlands and poisoned water sources. The pace of change would have varied, but in certain areas and at certain times it would have been highly visible over individual lifespans and must have been very traumatic for Mesolithic people.

Animals in the Mesolithic

Our knowledge of what animals existed in the Mesolithic comes mainly from the excavation of a small number of sites where bones survive in the archaeological record. Star Carr provides a great deal of this data. From these bones we know that people were hunting a broad range of species.

The larger species of animals present during the Mesolithic were red and roe deer, wild cattle (known as aurochs), elk, wild pig and bear. Some of these wild animals can still be found in parts of Europe though aurochs are now extinct, the last known animal being recorded in Poland in the 17th century AD. There were also a number of other animals including wolf, red fox, wild cat, lynx, badger, otter, beaver, pine marten, polecat, stoat, weasel, wood mouse, four species of vole (bank, field, root and water), dormouse, red squirrel, mountain hare, mole, and three species of shrew (common, pygmy and water).

Birds have been recorded from a number of sites and include great auk, razorbill, guillemot, cormorant, puffin, gull, goose, white-tailed eagle, whooper swan, crane, white stork, grebe, lapwing, buzzard and duck. These birds would have provided food, fat, oil, skin, feathers and bone; even a bead made from bird bone has been found at Star Carr.

In freshwater environments pike and perch would have been fished. At coastal sites many other species of fish have been found including herring, gurnard, mackerel, wrasse, halibut, saithe, eel, sturgeon, salmon, trout, cod, haddock and turbot. At coastal sites we also often find evidence that people were collecting shellfish, either to eat or for bait. In Britain the main species were limpet, cockle, periwinkle and oyster depending on location.

At many of these coastal sites we find deposits which we call shell middens.

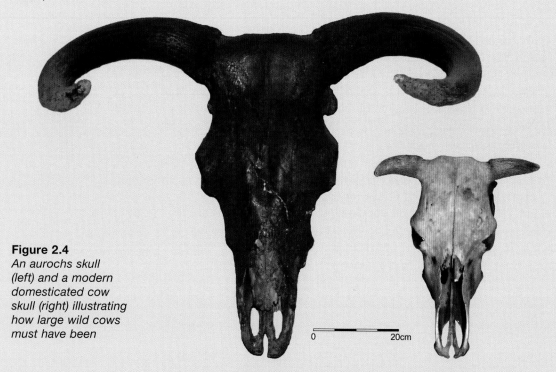

Figure 2.4
An aurochs skull (left) and a modern domesticated cow skull (right) illustrating how large wild cows must have been

0   20cm

Figure 2.5
A dog burial from the late Mesolithic site of Skateholm, Sweden

Middens are rubbish dumps, and these sites include thousands of shells – the remains of meals. In amongst the shell debris we often find a range of other food waste such as fish bone and animal bone and at some sites stone and bone tools or other artefacts are also found within the shell matrix. Like peat, shell middens have the capacity to stop organic materials deteriorating: the shell is made of calcium carbonate which is highly alkaline and this helps neutralise acidic soils which would usually erode away the bone. Shell middens are therefore very useful sites for providing evidence of past diet and subsistence.

We have to remember that in different environments people would have eaten very different diets. In addition, the changing environment through time would have had an impact on ecosystems. For instance, the elk appears to become much rarer after the start of the Mesolithic which is probably related to the increase of denser forests. At present, we have so few sites with plentiful bone remains that it is very hard to determine change through time, but with the discovery of more sites in the future, we will be able to look for evidence of both changing animal populations and changing diets.

Finally, it is important to note that there was one domesticated animal in the Mesolithic: the dog. The dog was domesticated from the grey wolf during the Palaeolithic period and appears at a number of Mesolithic sites in Britain including Star Carr. It was probably used in hunting but people may have had special connections with these animals: at Mesolithic sites in Sweden, the Netherlands and Portugal graves have been found with dog burials within them. While other animals had not been domesticated in this period, it is possible that people were trying to tame some species. At a site in France, the jaw of a young bear has been found which has very distinctive notches on it, suggestive that a bit had been placed in the cub's mouth from a very young age.

Figure 2.6
(a) Archaeologist Phil Harding knapping flint; (b) a Mesolithic flint core

Technology

People had a rich environment in which to live but they needed to develop technology in order to exploit it. In an age before the discovery of metal, stone was fundamental for their everyday lives because it enabled them to make weapons for hunting, blades for cutting and axes for chopping, amongst other things. This is why this period is called the Stone Age, but other materials were also of critical importance; in particular, in this period we see the development of wood-working.

Making stone tools

On the vast majority of Mesolithic sites the main type of evidence found is worked stone. As early as 3.4 million years ago in the Palaeolithic, it had been known that a flake of stone could have a very sharp edge, useful in all sorts of jobs from cutting up meat to making things out of other materials like bone, antler and hide. By the Mesolithic, people had developed their stone-knapping skills to produce a range of tools and weapons such as arrows, knives, axes, scrapers and borers.

People used several different types of stone for their tools depending on availability, but generally flint was used where possible because it is particularly sharp and flakes in a predictable fashion. Flint is a sedimentary form of quartz which occurs naturally in chalk. It appears as nodules which have a chalky exterior but inside the stone is usually grey or brown and often has a glassy appearance.

Knapping is the term used for shaping stone into tools by hitting it. When a nodule of flint is struck by another hard object it splits into thin, sharp splinters which are known as flakes and blades. Hard stones can be used as hammers, or softer materials such as antler tines can be used which will generally produce thinner flakes and blades. Striking a nodule of flint requires a lot of practice and should not be attempted without some guidance: the flakes and splinters that are broken off are sharper than surgical steel and can cause serious injury.

The piece of flint which is being knapped is known as the core. This core may be struck over and over again in order to produce a large number of blades or flakes but at some point it will be discarded when it stops producing good splinters. These cores are often found on Mesolithic sites and demonstrate that flint knapping has actually taken place on the site.

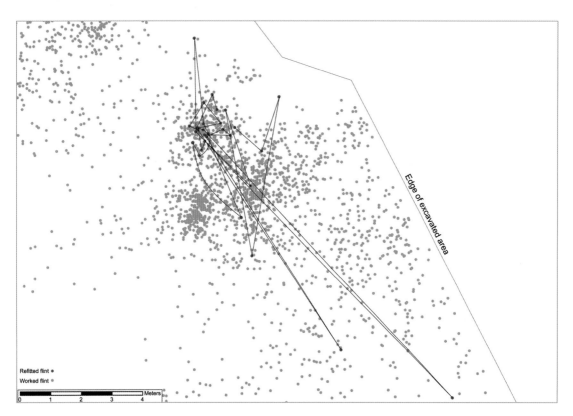

Figure 2.7 *Plan showing refitting flints*

A flake is simply a piece of stone detached through knapping; a blade is a flake with parallel sides and twice as long as it is wide. It is possible to identify whether a piece of flint has been deliberately struck because there will be evidence of the striking platform (where the blow was delivered), the bulb of percussion (where the force from the blow moves into the flint), and usually, depending on the material, there are ripples radiating from the striking platform which show the direction of the force as the flake was detached. Although these flakes are very sharp and extremely useful for cutting, some of them would have been discarded; such flakes are known as debitage. Others underwent a further sequence of shaping and 'retouching' that turned them into tools.

Archaeologists study stone tools in order to understand what knapping processes took place and where. Sometimes it is possible to carry out a refitting programme, which entails fitting the waste flakes and tools back together again to reconstruct the original like an enormous 3D jigsaw puzzle, though it is a jigsaw that is missing the picture and only includes half the pieces! Although this is extremely time consuming, it allows a detailed reconstruction of the methods people used to work flint and their thought processes and decisions when knapping. It also allows archaeologists to study the location of manufacturing and how tools were moved around and used in different parts of the site and in the broader landscape, enabling them to paint a detailed picture of people's movements. Refitting has been used on Stone Age sites to look at the sharing and ownership of tools and food, as well identifying apprentices learning the skill of flint knapping from a specialist stone-worker.

Over the past 30 years we have started to build up a better picture of how tools were used by looking at microscopic scratches (known as use-wear) that have been left on the flint. These can be matched to different types of material, such as bone, wood, or plant fibres and can also show us whether the flint was used for slicing, sawing or scraping. This analysis has shown that tools often had a variety of uses and that we should be careful about assigning a specific function to a particular type of tool. It has also shown that many of the sharp but unmodified flakes and blades which were created when knapping flint were used as cutting and scraping tools themselves.

Other materials

While flint tools provide most of the evidence for Mesolithic technology, we know that people were also manufacturing and using artefacts from a range of other materials, such as plants, bone, and antler. As we have already seen, because these materials are organic they decay relatively quickly, and tend not to survive on most archaeological sites. In some cases, however, such objects have been preserved, either in waterlogged sediments or calcareous-rich environments, and provide a tantalising glimpse of the full range of Mesolithic artefacts and technologies.

Mesolithic people were accomplished carpenters and, as in today's world, many of the objects that people used would have been made from wood. Perhaps the most important for day-to-day survival were hunting tools such as bows and arrows, and spears. Bow and arrow technology had existed in Europe since the late Palaeolithic and continued to be used throughout the Mesolithic. Discoveries of bows or arrows are few and far between but we have already seen an example of a complete arrow with microliths embedded in a wooden shaft. These wooden shafts would have been worked using flint tools and were sometimes heated in a fire to straighten them to ensure an accurate flight trajectory when fired. A few examples of bows have also been discovered in waterlogged

The Mesolithic tool kit

The flint artefact which is most associated with the Mesolithic is the microlith, a small tool made from a notched and snapped flint blade. Microliths would not have been used individually, but would have been hafted in groups onto a piece of bone, antler or wood, using birch resin or other adhesives to keep the flints in place. This incredibly versatile technology allowed Mesolithic people to produce a wide range of tools that could be used for a variety of tasks.

The tool most commonly associated with microliths is the arrow, which could be made by placing the flints along the edge and on the tip of a long wooden shaft. One example of microliths used in this way was recorded at Rönneholms in Sweden. Microliths were also used to create other tools, such as knives, piercers, sickles or saws.

Figure 2.8 *A selection of Mesolithic microliths*

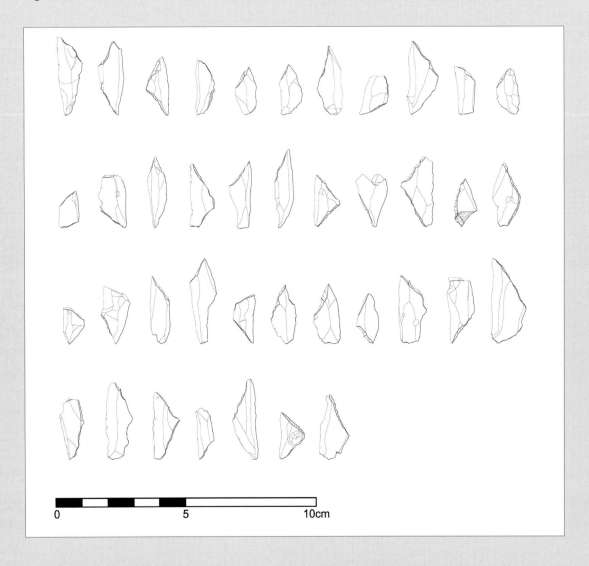

Figure 2.9 *The remains of an arrow made from hafted microliths found at Rönneholms Mosse, Sweden. The microliths had been fitted into a groove that had been cut into the wooden shaft, and were held in place using resin*

Figure 2.10 *An early Mesolithic tranchet axe discovered during excavations at Flixton Island in the Vale of Pickering*

grooves into antler, whilst scrapers have a blunted end and may have been used for scraping animal hides.

The production of stone tools develops and changes through time and in different regions. Although there are many similarities in tool manufacture across the Early Mesolithic in Europe, there are also variations. For instance, in the Early Mesolithic, people produced microliths which were made on broad blades and in the Late Mesolithic, microliths become smaller and are geometric in shape. There are also variations in microlith form which are given different names after sites. So, for instance, in the Early Mesolithic there are 'Star Carr', 'Deepcar' and 'Horsham' microlith styles. These date to slightly different times in the Early Mesolithic and vary regionally. It has been suggested that these different styles of microliths reflect the traditions of groups of people who were moving back into Britain from different parts of Europe at the start of the Mesolithic.

Another significant, though often overlooked, flint tool is the axe. It was made by working a piece of flint into an oval shape and then removing a large flake from one end to create the cutting edge. Axes made in this way are known as 'tranchet axes', and would have been hafted and used for cutting and working wood. They first appear in the Early Mesolithic period and herald the beginnings of wood-working.

As well as axes and microliths, Mesolithic people made a range of other tools out of flint. Archaeologists have assigned specific functions to some of these tools, based on the way the flint has been shaped. Burins, for example, have a pointed end and are thought to have been used for scoring

environments at a number of Mesolithic sites. The oldest known Mesolithic bows are from the site of Holmegaard in Denmark where the remains of five bows were found, all made of elm.

Wood was also used to make boats as well as hunting equipment. Excavations in Denmark and Holland have discovered dug-out canoes made from the trunks of lime trees that had been shaped and hollowed using stone axes. Many of these canoes are very large: one is almost 10m long and could have carried around eight people. It is likely that it was used for transportation and fishing by communities living on the coast or along rivers. Wooden paddles have also been found, some of which have been decorated.

People living along the coast or close to rivers or lakes during the Mesolithic also used wood to make traps for eels and fish. These consist of thin pieces of wood woven together to make large conical baskets that were placed under the water. Fish or eels swimming into these baskets would become trapped, and the baskets could then be collected. Spectacular examples of these baskets have been discovered by archaeologists working in Denmark, Holland and, recently, in Ireland, and the widespread distribution of these finds suggests that the technology necessary to make and use fish traps was relatively commonplace. In Denmark these sorts of traps are generally thought to be used for trapping eels, but people may have used them to catch other types of fish too.

Wood was also an important building material during the Mesolithic. In the past 50 years, a number of large round

Figure 2.12 *(facing page) A fish trap from Clowanstown, County Meath, in the Republic of Ireland during excavation*

Figure 2.13
*Reconstruction
of the Mesolithic
structure discovered
during excavations
at Howick in
Northumberland*

The Mesolithic

structures or buildings have been discovered at sites in Britain and Ireland. Even though wood does not survive at these sites, the holes that would have held timber posts have been recorded and these show that that the buildings were supported by wooden frames. Archaeologists have reconstructed one of these buildings at Howick, Northumberland, using the floor plan of the original Mesolithic structure. Although it is difficult to tell exactly what this building would have looked like, the Howick reconstruction does provide a sense of how such structures would have been built and what it would have been like to live in them.

Not everything made from wood, however, had a practical purpose: one of the most incredible examples of wood-working is a wooden 'idol' found in a peat bog at Shigir (in the Urals in Russia) in 1894 which dates to about 7500 BC. It is several metres tall and is carved with a head at the top and a number of faces all over the body. Unfortunately we do not know what its original purpose was, but it is tempting to see it as something similar to a totem pole or possibly the representation of an important spirit.

In addition to wood, people also made good use of other plant materials. Containers made from birch bark have been discovered on several Mesolithic sites, and there is evidence that plant fibres were used to make ropes and twine which could be fashioned into nets, mats or baskets.

Although Mesolithic people were not farmers, some archaeologists have argued that they controlled the growth of certain plants in order to provide reliable sources of food or raw materials. Perhaps the most convincing evidence is for coppicing, the practice of cutting down a young tree close to its base in order to promote the growth of long straight stems. These stems have a very distinctive growth pattern, and artefacts from several Mesolithic sites appear to have been manufactured from wood that has been grown in this way. However, coppice can also occur naturally, and it is unclear whether the wood that was being used by Mesolithic people was the result of intentional woodland management. There is also evidence for the deliberate burning of vegetation,

Figure 2.14
The Shigir idol

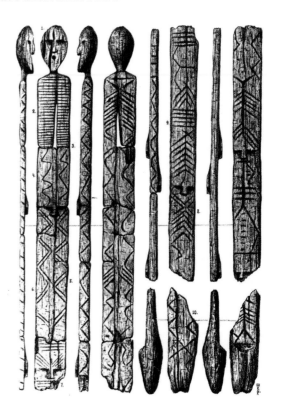

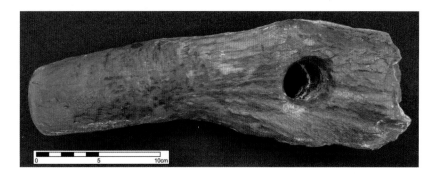

Figure 2.15 *An axe made from a piece of elk antler*

particularly reed beds growing around the edges of lakes. This is thought to have been carried out to remove invasive plant species and promote the growth of taller, healthier plants that could then be collected and used as raw materials.

People also used a range of animal products for things other than food, some of which we have examples of and some of which we can presume. For instance, sinews would have been useful for tying: we do not find the sinews themselves in the archaeological record but we have evidence from marks on animal bones that people were removing them.

Antler, particularly from red deer, is commonly used in the Mesolithic. Artefacts made from antler include barbed points or harpoons (as found at Star Carr) which would have been used in hunting and fishing, and axes which may have been used in wood-working. Elk antler was also utilised to make mattocks, which might have been used for digging up roots or tubers, or perhaps for digging pits or postholes.

Another material used for making tools was bone. Bone fish hooks have been found at several Danish Mesolithic coastal sites and in Scotland a large number of 'bevel-ended tools' have been found in shell midden sites. These are splinters of bone which have a rounded, worked end. It is thought that this end would have been used for scraping hides to help soften them, presumably in preparation for making clothing. We don't have any direct evidence for clothing but at the Palaeolithic sites of Robin Hood's Cave (Derbyshire) and Gough's Cave (Somerset) bone needles have been found, suggesting people did sew and mend. We also know that people ornamented their clothes or wore jewellery, as beads have been found at a number of sites. The area around Nab Head in south Wales appears to have been a manufacturing centre for beads made out of shale disks and around 700 are known from the site. Similar beads are found on other sites across south Wales and in northern England (including Star Carr).

Human behaviour

Settlement and mobility

The traditional view of hunter-gatherers is that they lived in relatively small groups and moved from place to place, often on a seasonal basis, as they followed migrating herds of animals or exploited resources that were only available at certain times of the year. This perception certainly seems to hold true for the Early Mesolithic in Europe, where many sites appear to be very small in size and so have been thought to represent the temporary settlements of small, highly mobile groups.

In recent years, however, we have begun to find many more 'houses' on Mesolithic sites which seem to suggest an alternative view to the idea that people were highly mobile. One of these was recently discovered at Howick, in Northumberland, and provides us with a very detailed record of the building of structures during the Mesolithic. The structure itself is about 6m across, and consists of a large hollow surrounded by holes that would have held wooden posts. In the centre of the house were a number of hearths one above another, each containing large quantities of burnt hazelnut shells. By dating these in sequence it was possible through statistical modelling to say that the house must have been occupied for at least 100 years. There was also evidence that it was rebuilt or mended several times, with the insertion of new posts. This is significant because it shows that some houses were maintained for several generations, which clearly indicates that people felt a strong link with particular places in the landscape.

This is not to say that people always stayed in one place. For example, the study of stone tools from a number of Scottish sites has provided good evidence of mobility in this region. Here flint is not so common so Mesolithic people knapped a wide variety of stone types. Some of these are particularly distinctive and restricted to very localised areas, such as the Rum bloodstone. Consequently, when Mesolithic tools made of Rum bloodstone are found a long way from source, it demonstrates they have moved long distances, either as a result of movement of people, or as some form of trade or gift giving.

In other regions detailed archaeological work has begun to build up a picture of the spatial organisation of different activities across an area. In the early part of the Mesolithic, people often camped along the River Kennet, a tributary of the Thames. Some sites were used for hunting red deer; at others pigs were the main

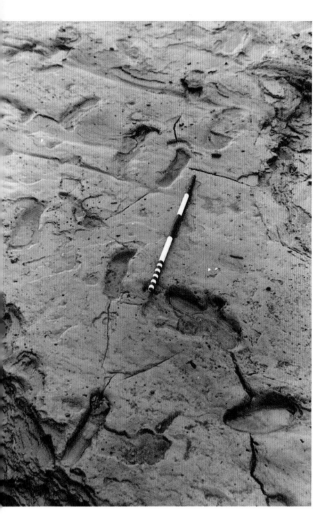

Figure 2.16
Footprint-tracks of two people at Goldcliff East in the Severn Estuary. The narrow tracks are probably those of a young child. These tracks frequently cross those of the larger, adult prints, suggesting the child may have been running around

prey animal; hazelnuts were also collected and processed along the river. The stone tools found at different sites also show that activities varied: at some sites tools were repaired and at others tasks such as bone-, antler- and hide-working were carried out.

One of the most intimate accounts of Mesolithic life comes from the Severn Estuary, where human and animal footprints have been discovered preserved in layers of estuarine sediments. By studying the sizes of the individual footprints and the distances between them archaeologists have been able to estimate the age and height of the individuals who made them, and have used this information to identify the tracks of 21 separate people. They have also been able to tell if people were walking or running, and if they were travelling alone or in small groups.

In one case, the tracks were made by a group of four people, all walking together at a similar pace and in the same direction. At one point, the group paused, perhaps to check their bearings or to watch for animals. Deer tracks were also present in this area and it is possible that this group of people were hunting. In another case the tracks were made by two people, a young child (aged between 3 and 4) and an older individual (10 or 11 years old), who may have been playing.

Diet and subsistence

One of the most important, and potentially difficult questions relating to life in the prehistoric past is 'what did people eat?'. Mesolithic people employed a number of different strategies when hunting animals. For example, the large and potentially dangerous mammals, such as aurochs, would have been hunted using projectiles like arrows and spears that were tipped with bone or antler points or flint microliths. In some cases, the remains of

Figure 2.17 *An early Mesolithic stone hearth discovered during excavations at Seamer Carr in the Vale of Pickering*

these weapons have been found amongst the bones of the animals, and in others there is evidence for the injuries that led to the animal's death. In contrast, smaller mammals may have been hunted using traps or snares that were set along paths or outside burrows. This technique would have been particularly important when hunting fur-bearing animals, such as pine marten, as it would allow the animal to be captured without damaging its precious pelt. Birds were probably sought for their feathers as well as their meat. These may have been hunted with wooden-tipped arrows, in order not to damage the feathers, as done by many hunter-gatherer groups today.

As well as meat and fish, wild plants also formed an important part of people's diet. Although these leave little trace in the archaeological record, excavations at Mesolithic sites across Northern Europe have recorded a broad range of plant foods, including hazelnuts, wild berries, the tubers of the herb lesser celandine, water lily seeds, and nuts of the shrub common dogwood, as well as a variety of wild grasses and sedges. In some cases there is also evidence for the processing of these plants. For instance, at the Early Mesolithic site of Duvensee, in North Germany, archaeologists discovered the remains of hearths that had been used to roast hazelnuts, and similar discoveries have been made on sites in Britain and Ireland. Large stones, thought to have been used for grinding, have also been discovered and may have been used to create a kind of flour or to extract oil from the nuts of plants such as the common dogwood.

We have very little evidence for the way food was prepared,

The Mesolithic   33 though we assume that people cooked over hearths or by placing food into covered pits containing hot stones or smouldering fires. Water may also have been poured into pits or tightly woven baskets and then heated with hot stones. When an animal such as a red deer, aurochs or elk was killed it would have produced large quantities of meat and it is possible that people had the expertise to smoke or dry it, so that it would not have gone to waste; alternatively the killing of large animals may have been an excuse for a feast!

Death

The study of burial practices in the past is one of the most fascinating aspects of archaeological research and can tell us much about a society's attitude to death and the afterlife. We know from excavations that have been carried out in other parts of Northern Europe that Mesolithic people treated their dead in a variety of ways. At some sites, bodies were placed in graves, a practice known as inhumation, and were accompanied with artefacts, such as stone tools, beads and animal remains. At other sites, bodies were cremated on funeral pyres and the burnt remains interred in pits. There is also evidence that dead bodies were deliberately de-fleshed and then dismembered, either by using stone tools or by leaving the corpse to decay, and that the remains were then either interred in special places in the landscape or taken away by people. Although such practices seem very unusual to us, they appear to have played an important part in Mesolithic communities and may have been associated with the veneration of ancestors or of other important people.

Unfortunately the evidence we have from Britain is very sparse, particularly in comparison with other parts of Northern Europe, and often consists of just single bones or small groups of bones. Most of these have been found in caves, particularly on the Gower Peninsula in Wales, and the Mendip Hills in south-west England, though single bones have been found at the Early Mesolithic settlement site at Thatcham in Berkshire, and in an ancient river channel at Staythorpe in Derbyshire. Some archaeologists have argued that these finds are evidence for practices that involved de-fleshing and dismemberment similar to those that took place in other parts of Europe. Perhaps the best evidence we have for this comes from Oronsay in Scotland, where human bones were found within shell middens. Some of these were found in small clusters and may have been gathered together and deliberately

Figure 2.18 *(a) The pit containing the cremated remains of a body that was discovered during excavations at Hermitage, Castleconnell (the Republic of Ireland); (b) the stone axe that had been interred with the remains*

deposited after the bodies had been de-fleshed. Although the remains of several individuals were present, the skulls and long bones were missing, suggesting these may have been taken away by people and left in other parts of the landscape.

These practices of de-fleshing and dismemberment were not the only forms of burial in Britain and Ireland. Evidence for the cremation of bodies has recently been discovered during excavations at the site of Hermitage, in Castleconnell, Ireland, where the cremated remains of two individuals had been interred in separate pits. In one of these, the cremation was accompanied by several artefacts, including a stone axe, all of which had been burnt, and are thought to have been placed on the funeral pyre along with the body of the deceased. The only complete Mesolithic inhumation was discovered in Gough's Cave in Cheddar Gorge at the start of the 20th century. While these discoveries of inhumation and cremation burials are very rare, it is possible that the practices were far more widespread in the Mesolithic and that the burials have simply become disturbed or destroyed by later activity. This may explain the presence of small groups of human bones that have been found in caves.

The only British site large enough to be thought of as a cemetery was discovered in a cave, known as Aveline's Hole, in Somerset, England. Unfortunately the site was first discovered at the end of the 18th century and subsequent visitors to the cave disturbed and removed some of the bones, leaving little record of what had been found. The site was excavated in the first half of the 20th century, but the excavation records and many of the

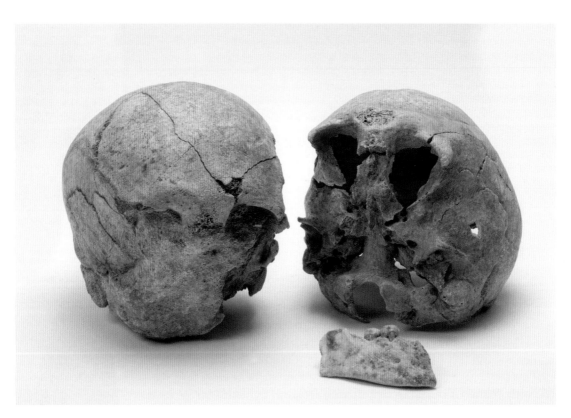

Figure 2.19 *Skulls from Greylake, Somerset*

finds were destroyed during the Second World War. As a result we don't know how many people were interred in the cave, how the bodies were laid out, whether they were all complete, and what sorts of objects were placed around them. Recent analysis of the surviving material, however, has shown that perhaps as many as 50 individuals were brought into the cave, whilst radiocarbon dating has shown that the burials date to the Early Mesolithic.

Recently, re-dating of human remains from another site in southern England has provided further evidence for Mesolithic burials. In the 1920s a small collection of human remains, including five skulls and several long bones, was discovered during quarrying at the site of Greylake, in the Somerset Levels. Some of the remains were subsequently lost, but two of the skulls were recently radiocarbon dated to the Early Mesolithic. Currently, it is not clear whether these were complete burials or disarticulated humans but the fact that finger bones were found in the sand cleaned out of the skulls implies the latter. Interestingly, Greylake would have been a small island during the Mesolithic; it is possible that this made the site a significant place in the landscape and thus a suitable location to inter the dead.

Beliefs and rituals

Sometimes the archaeological material discovered cannot easily be interpreted in terms of people's day-to-day tasks such as hunting or tool production, and seems to suggest ritual or religious practices. Whilst we may be able to identify such activities, it is much harder to understand the motivations behind them, simply on the basis of the archaeology alone. Instead, we need to look at ethnographic accounts of modern or recent hunter-gatherers in order to understand their beliefs and the ways in which artefacts are used and deposited in ritual activities.

For example, the Siberian Khanty observe certain traditions when consuming different animals in order to nurture relationships with the supernatural beings that control particular animal species. The elk is regarded as a clean animal and the remains are disposed of in clean areas of the forest away from disturbance by dogs. Bears are also considered important and their remains are placed in deep pools of water. Several archaeological excavations have recorded artefacts and animal remains in lakes or pools of water, which may reflect similar practices to those carried out by the Khanty.

It is also possible that shamans existed in Mesolithic societies. Shamans are people who are intermediaries with the spirit world and communicate with the spirits through altered states of consciousness, often entering into a trance. This practice is recorded in a number of ethnographic accounts around the world and it is thought to originate as far back as the Palaeolithic. Such practices are difficult to identify archaeologically, but excavations at several sites have recorded features which have been interpreted as the burial of a shaman. At Bad Dürrenberg in Germany, rescue excavations in the 1930s discovered an adult woman buried in a seated position and accompanied by a large number of unusual grave goods. These included pieces of tortoiseshell, a bone container holding microliths, and a large number of pendants made from animal teeth that the woman had been wearing. As well as the unusual grave goods, recent analysis has identified pathologies on the bones that may have caused the woman to experience spasms and other neurological complaints. These issues, some archaeologists have suggested, would have marked the woman out as different and may have been interpreted by other members of her society as being related to shamanistic practices.

Interestingly, the evidence from Bad Dürrenberg has parallels with a burial found in Israel, which dates to around 10,000 BC.

Vedbaek

The site of Vedbaek in Denmark dates to around 4000 BC and is one of the most well-known Mesolithic burial sites in Europe. The cemetery was first discovered in 1975 by amateur archaeologists in advance of the building of a school. Once graves containing skeletons were found an archaeological investigation was begun which soon revealed a cemetery. What is surprising is that there had been four earlier excavations at this site but all had missed the burials!

A total of seventeen graves were investigated but it is likely that more had been destroyed by building works. The graves themselves were all trough-shaped oval holes in the ground between 0.5m and 1m below the original surface; they appear to have been laid out in parallel rows.

Most of the graves contained only one individual but some held two or three people. The excavators thought that the bodies had probably been buried fully dressed, judging from the position of the grave goods. There were a number of different types of grave goods, including red deer antlers, stone and bone tools and beads. The beads were mainly made out of animal teeth, in particular wild pig, red deer, and aurochs, and there were even three human teeth! Red ochre, a natural red powdery stone, had been ground up and scattered in all of the graves.

In one of the graves (grave number 8) there was a large heap of pendants (190 altogether) and perforated snail shells by the head of a woman. More snail shells were found under the pelvis, along with a row of about 50 tooth pendants. It is thought that a dress or item of clothing may have been represented by the heap at her head, and the shells round her waist might have been stitched onto clothing she was buried in. Several of the graves, including number 8, had a baby burial along with the adult. In this instance the baby had been laid to rest on a swan's wing.

The attention that has been given to the burials both on this site and others demonstrates that people in the Mesolithic cared for their dead. We have no way of knowing whether they believed in an afterlife, though it is possible that the grave goods were placed alongside the bodies in order to equip them for the next world.

Figure 2.20 *The burial of a young woman and a newborn baby (grave 8). The baby had been laid out on a swan's wing*

The burial was that of a small, old woman who had been interred with a unique set of grave goods. These included 50 complete tortoiseshells, body parts from a number of animals including an eagle and a leopard, and even a complete human foot. In this case, some archaeologists have suggested that the woman was a shaman because many of these offerings are used in shamanistic practices today.

There is also evidence that people built structures that marked out special places in the landscape. The most substantial of these was discovered at Warren Field in Aberdeenshire where excavations recorded a line of at least twelve large pits, extending for a distance of over 50m. Four large pits of Mesolithic date were also found during excavations at Stonehenge, whilst several others have been found at other sites across England and Wales. Although the function of these pits and 'pit alignments' is not known, archaeologists believe that they may have been used to denote significant places, where people came together and, possibly, where rituals or ceremonies were carried out. In the case of the Stonehenge pits, these would have held large timber posts and it is tempting to think that these may have been carved in a similar manner to the Shigir idol.

Conclusions

When we piece together the evidence from European Mesolithic archaeology we can begin to glimpse a picture of hunter-gatherer life between 9600 and 4000 BC. In the past there has been a tendency in Mesolithic archaeology to assume that everything was the same over this 5600-year period, but it is clear there were many differences both in how people lived and what they did, depending on where they were living and at what moment in time. However, there are still many gaps in our knowledge and lots of questions which might usefully be researched, particularly in Britain. Star Carr has enabled us to understand a lot more about this period because of the organic artefacts that have been discovered, but as we will see in the next chapter, recent studies have also produced a whole new set of questions.

Suggested further reading

If you want to learn more about the British and European Mesolithic, the following books all provide a good summary of the period. Full details may be found in the Bibliography.

The archaeology of Britain: An introduction from earliest times to the twenty-first century, edited by John Hunter and Ian Ralston

Prehistoric Britain, by Timothy Darvill

The Oxford Illustrated History of Prehistoric Europe, edited by Barry Cunliffe

For a global perspective, try:

After the Ice. A global human history, by Steven Mithen

For more information about the Palaeolithic sites mentioned in this chapter try:

The British Palaeolithic: Hominin societies on the edge of the Pleistocene world, by Paul Pettitt and Mark White

For more detailed information about the Mesolithic period, focusing either on particular geographic locations or particular aspects of the past, the following books provide a good starting point.

Mesolithic Britain and Ireland: New Approaches, edited by Chantal Conneller and Graeme Warren

Mesolithic Scotland and its Neighbours, edited by Alan Saville

Stone Age Hunters of the British Isles, by Christopher Smith

Mesolithic Lives in Scotland, by Graeme Warren

Prehistoric Coastal Communities: the Mesolithic in western Britain, by Martin Bell

Mesolithic Europe, edited by Geoff Bailey and Penny Spikins

Europe's Lost World. The rediscovery of Doggerland, by Vince Gaffney, Simon Fitch and David Smith

Mesolithic settlement in the North Sea basin. A case study from Howick, north-east England, edited by C Waddington

The Skateholm project: a late Mesolithic settlement and cemetery complex at a southern Swedish bay, by L Larsson

Mesolithic research in the bog Rönneholms mosse, southern Sweden, by L Larsson & S Sjöström

An early Mesolithic seasonal hunting site in the Kennet Valley, southern England, by C Ellis, J Allen, J Gardiner, P Harding, C Ingrem, A Powell & R Scaife

Rhum, Mesolithic and later sites at Kinloch, excavations 1984–1986, by C Wickham-Jones

Hazelnut ecologies of early Holocene hunter-gatherers: a case study from Duvensee, by D Holst

Excavations on Oronsay: prehistoric human ecology on a small island, by P Mellars

Fire and water ... Early Mesolithic cremations at Hermitage, Co. Limerick, by T Collins & F Coyne

'...pursuing a rabbit in Burrington Combe'. New research on the early Mesolithic burial cave of Aveline's Hole, by R J Schulting

An early Mesolithic cemetery at Greylake, Somerset, UK, by R Brunning & H Firth

The Burial of Bad Dürrenberg, central Germany: osteopathology and osteoarchaeology of a late Mesolithic shaman's grave, by M Porr & K W Alt

Excavation of a Mesolithic cemetery at Vedbaek, Denmark, by S E Albrethsen & E Brinch Petersen

A tale of the unknown unknowns: a Mesolithic pit alignment and a Neolithic timber hall at Warren Field, Crathes, Aberdeenshire, by H K Murray, J C Murray & M F Shannon

And for a very personal account of Mesolithic archaeology try:

To the Islands: An Archaeologist's Relentless Quest to Find the Prehistoric Hunter-Gatherers of the Hebrides, by Steven Mithen

These publications provide a good (though sometimes quite technical) introduction to the causes and effects of past climatic and environmental change and the methods that are used to record them.

An Environmental History of Great Britain: from 10,000 Years Ago to the Present, by Ian Simmonds

Late Quaternary Environmental Change. Physical and Human Perspectives, by Martin Bell and Michael Walker

Reconstructing Quaternary Environments, by John Lowe and Mike Walker

Finally, several writers have provided fictional accounts of life in the Mesolithic, which draw heavily on the archaeological evidence from sites including Star Carr.

Mezolith, by Ben Haggarty and Adam Brockbank

The Gathering Night, by Margaret Elphinstone

The Chronicles of Ancient Darkness series, by Michelle Paver

Star Carr: the history of discoveries

3

Introduction

The story of the discovery of Star Carr starts with John Moore from Scarborough. He is the hero of the story: without him, the site of Star Carr might never have been found. Not only that, he also found nine other sites nearby and was the first person to identify that there had been a lake in the area. However, it is Grahame Clark who is most closely associated with Star Carr, as it was he who excavated the site from 1949 until 1951. More recently, further work has been carried out in the 1980s and the 2000s under the auspices of the Vale of Pickering Research Trust. This chapter describes the fieldwork undertaken and the key discoveries that have been made.

John Moore

Unfortunately, we know very little about John Moore. He lived in Scarborough in the 1940s and was one of a group of keen enthusiasts who, in 1947, set up the 'Scarborough and District Archaeological Society' (now known as the 'Scarborough Archaeological and Historical Society') in order to preserve and research the rich archaeological inheritance of the area.

In the 1940s, there were no obvious indications on the surface that there had been a lake in the past so, in order to understand the ancient land surface, Moore took numerous borings over the fields, allowing him to map the underlying topography beneath the peat. Moore realised the peat had formed within a now extinct

Figure 3.1
John Moore

Figure 3.2 *The location of the sites discovered by John Moore around Lake Flixton*

lake which he named Lake Flixton. In 1951 he wrote an account of this work, 'Lake Flixton: a Late-Glacial Structure', in the first publication of the Scarborough and District Archaeological Society.

As well as recording the lake, Moore also looked for evidence of human activity around its shores. To do this he began to examine the peat deposits that had been exposed in recently cut ditches as well as looking for artefacts in the ploughsoil on the higher ground where the peat was much thinner. In 1947 he discovered a single flint blade at the base of the peat in one of the ditches, and in the following year he excavated a trench across the adjacent area where he recorded a dense concentration of Early Mesolithic flint. Moore referred to this as Site 1, but it is now known as Flixton Island; it was the first hint of prehistoric activity around the lake.

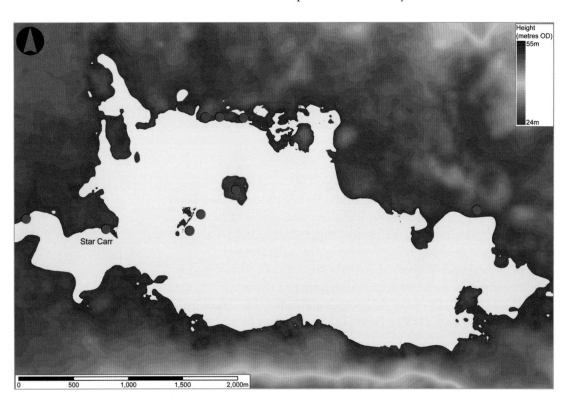

Star Carr

Height (metres OD)
55m
24m

0   500   1,000   1,500   2,000m

In 1948 Moore conducted further work in the fields immediately to the north and found a second site (Flixton Site 2). As well as recording more evidence of Mesolithic activity Moore also discovered the remains of at least three horses 'of moderate proportions' in a much lower layer of peat. In 1948 Dr Harry Godwin (University of Cambridge) and Roy Clapham (then Professor of Botany at Sheffield University) visited Moore's excavations at Flixton and obtained a pollen core from the vicinity. Their work suggested that the sediments with horse bone were Late Palaeolithic in age, and probably formed during a warm phase towards the end of the last Ice Age.

Both Godwin, and the curator of the Scarborough Museum, Mr Gwatkin, persuaded Moore to discuss his findings with Grahame Clark, who was then a lecturer at the University of Cambridge. Clark had been looking for a Mesolithic site in Britain which was either in, or close to, a bog where organic materials, such as bone and antler might survive. Clark later wrote of his excitement on receiving a 'parcel of flints' from Moore which he initially assigned to the Maglemosian:

> It took only a glance to see that here was a clue to something I had been seeking for many years: that is, a flint industry, analogous to that first recognized by Danish archaeologists at Maglemose, Mullerup, on the island of Zealand, from a British locality offering promise of recovering a settlement site with organic as well as merely lithic data … my first question on establishing contact with Mr Moore was whether he had found antler or bone on any of his sites. On hearing that he had, I lost no time in meeting him.

Convinced that this location had the potential for further discoveries, Clark returned to the site in 1949 and carried out the first of three years of excavations. Moore referred to this area as Site 4.

We know little of Moore's later work. In 1951 he returned to Flixton Island and excavated several more trenches at Sites 1 and 2 and discovered a small fragment of barbed point, similar to the many which were being found at Star Carr in the same year. He also spent some time at Star Carr once Clark had finished, removing the baulks (unexcavated walls of earth between trenches) and cataloguing the finds.

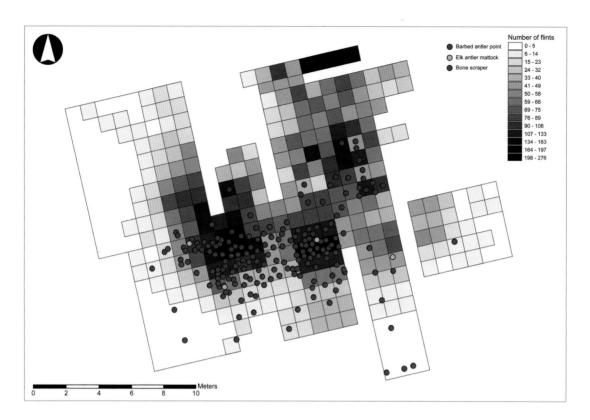

Figure 3.3 *The density of flint artefacts recorded by Grahame Clark and the distribution of some of the bone and antler artefacts*

Grahame Clark

The team

Dr Grahame Clark was 42 years old, and a lecturer at the University of Cambridge, when he first started work at Star Carr in 1949. He took undergraduates and research students from Cambridge to work with him, all of whom are listed in the acknowledgements of his book; many of these went on to be well-known archaeologists themselves. However, he also had some local people on the site from time to time including W H Lamplough and his son David, both well known locally for their extensive excavations of barrows on the North Yorkshire Moors.

Although Clark was working on a shoestring budget, he still managed to assemble a team of experts in the environmental sciences to help with various aspects of the project. These included Harry Godwin, Professor of Botany at Cambridge University, and Frederic Fraser and Judith King, from the Zoology department of the British Museum. This multidisciplinary approach to the study of the past had been pioneered by the Fenland Research

Committee, of which both Clark and Godwin had been members in the 1930s.

As Clark directed the excavations, Harry Godwin and Donald Walker carried out detailed studies of the peat and took samples which they analysed for pollen and other plant remains that had been preserved in the sediments. Using this data they were able to reconstruct the patterns of vegetation that existed at the time Star Carr was occupied and the nature of the environment within which the archaeological material had been deposited. They also carried out surveys of the surrounding area and created the first environmental history of the lake and the wider landscape.

The finds

In his first season at Star Carr, Clark excavated a single trench (referred to as a 'cutting') through the peat at the edge of the former lake. As they dug down through the peat, the excavators encountered a layer of birch branches, which they termed 'brushwood'. Clark interpreted this as a platform that had been laid down to stabilise the swamp deposits in order for people to inhabit the area. Although there was no evidence of structures on the brushwood, Clark did note that only the waterlogged parts of

Figure 3.4 (left) The 'brushwood' platform discovered during Grahame Clark's excavations at Star Carr

Figure 3.5 (right) The remains of the birch tree discovered by Grahame Clark

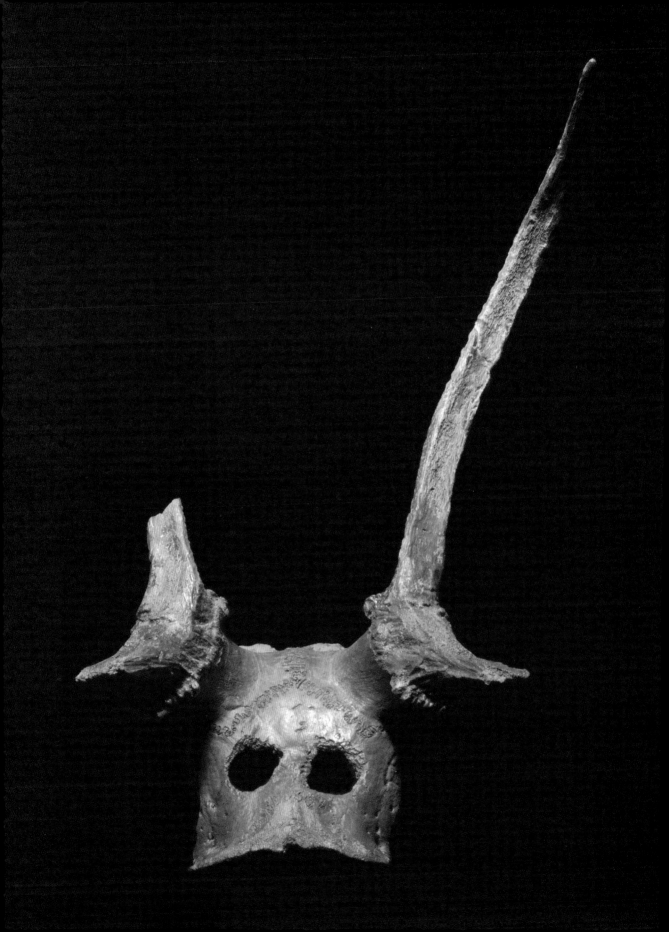

the platform survived, and if reed huts or skin tents had existed they would have decayed without trace.

In amongst the brushwood the excavators discovered an incredible wealth of archaeological material. As well as worked flint, to be expected on Mesolithic sites, there were large quantities of bone and antler artefacts, the butchered remains of animals, and waste material left over from making the antler objects. These were precisely the kinds of objects which Clark had hoped to find, and which have made Star Carr so important for our understanding of the Mesolithic in Britain. In the following years Clark and his team excavated further trenches through the edge of the former lake, exposing the extent of the brushwood platform and recording more of the bone and antler artefacts. They also discovered the remains of several trees, which Clark thought had been deliberately felled in order to clear paths through the reedswamp and create a 'primitive landing stage'.

The artefacts that Clark discovered at Star Carr were truly spectacular, in terms of both their number and the range of different objects. They are also incredibly rare, and to this day the material from Star Carr represents the single largest assemblage of bone and antler objects ever recorded on a British Early Mesolithic site.

Perhaps the most well known of the artefacts are the 21 worked stag frontlets. These had been made from the skulls of adult red deer, which had had the bones of the face and sides of the head removed. The inside of the skull had then been worked to make it smooth, holes had been cut through the bone at the back, and the antlers had been cut back and hollowed out. There are no other examples of such an artefact in Britain and only a few others are known on the Continent.

Figure 3.6 *Two of the red deer antler frontlets discovered at Star Carr*

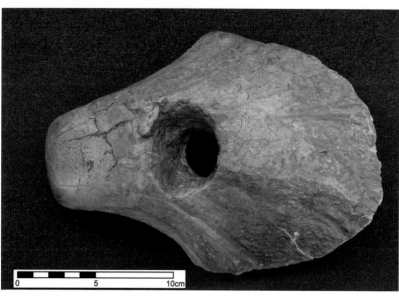

Figure 3.7 *Star Carr artefacts: (a) one of the 191 barbed antler points found at the site; (b) bodkins made from the metacarpal (foot bones) of an elk; (c) the head of a mattock made from a piece of elk antler; (d) a wooden paddle; (e) scraping tools made from the bones of an aurochs; (f) shale beads*

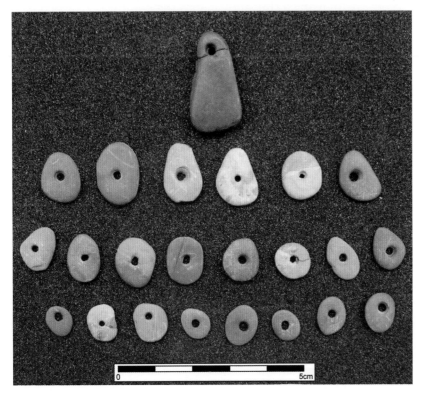

Based on the way they had been worked, Clark suggested that the frontlets had been worn as masks or head-dresses. In particular, he argued that the cutting and hollowing of the antler would have made the frontlets lighter and easier to wear, whilst the holes cut through the skull could have been used to tie the frontlet in place. Clark also suggested two possible functions for the frontlets: that they could have served either as a form of hunting disguise, which would allow the wearer to get closer to the deer without startling it, or that they were worn as a head-dress during ritual practices or dances. While both of these interpretations can be supported by data from the archaeological and anthropological record, Clark suggested that the frontlets had probably been used as a hunting disguise.

Clark also discovered 191 barbed antler points. These were also an incredible and rare find, and the assemblage from Star Carr constitutes over 80% of all Early Mesolithic barbed points known in Britain. The barbed antler points were made using a process we call 'groove and splinter'. This involves carving two parallel grooves along a piece of antler using a sharp flint cutting tool and then cutting out a thin strip, referred to as the splinter. The splinter was then whittled into the correct shape and the barbs cut out, again using a flint tool, before the point was attached to a wooden haft. One of the points found had a hole in its end and may have been used as a harpoon, whilst others may have been used as the tips of spears, javelins, or arrows. Points such as these can be used in a variety of ways for bringing down a range of animals from large game, such as deer or elk, to fish or beaver.

In addition to the barbed points, which were the most numerous antler tool found at the site, Clark discovered several other antler objects. These included red deer antler tines, which Clark thought had been worked to make scraping tools, and the heads of axes and mattocks made from elk antler. These had holes cut into them so they could be attached to a wooden handle, and in one case the burnt tip of the handle was still attached to the mattock head.

Clark also recorded a number of objects that had been made from animal bone. Amongst these were finely made bodkins, which had been worked from the metacarpal (front foot) bones of elk and may have been used as fastening pins, and scraping tools made from aurochs bone. The only piece of worked wood that was found was a small paddle. This was made from a piece of birch wood that had been whittled down using flint tools.

In addition to the objects, a large assemblage of animal bones was also recorded from the site which provided Clark with information on the species that the inhabitants of Star Carr had hunted. As well as large mammals, such as red and roe deer, elk, wild pig and wild cattle, smaller animals were also present. They included pine marten, fox, wolf, badger, hare, beaver and hedgehog. In a later reanalysis the bones of a domesticated dog and a brown bear were also identified. The bones of several different birds, such as common crane, red-breasted merganser and red-throated diver, were found on the site, species which would have been living on or around the lake during the time the site was occupied.

Clark's interpretation

The site was published in 1954, just three years after the end of the excavation, and it was only then that the site was renamed Star Carr. In his publication, Clark used the evidence provided by the artefacts, animal bones, and plant remains preserved in the peat to create a detailed reconstruction of life at Star Carr. To begin with, he argued that the site had been located in an area of reedswamp close to the edge of the lake. The 'brushwood' had been deliberately laid down to form an occupation surface on which people had lived; the artefacts and other materials had been lost or discarded by the inhabitants of the site. Based on the presence of hunting equipment and tools associated with domestic tasks such as hide scraping, Clark suggested that both men and women were living at the site, and that children were probably present too. Based on the size of the site he estimated the population of Star Carr to have been four or five families. On the basis of the number of animals that were represented by the bones, he also suggested that the site might have been occupied on several occasions for a period of about six years (though perhaps spread out over a long span of time). Finally, by calculating the time of year that some of the animals had been killed, he argued that the site had been inhabited during the winter. Almost 20 years later Clark expanded this interpretation when he tied Star Carr into a wider pattern of annual migration. This envisaged the inhabitants of Star Carr moving onto the surrounding hills during the summer months as they followed migrating herds of red deer, and then returning to the low-lying land around the lake in the winter.

Within a few years of the publication, Star Carr had become world famous in the discipline of archaeology. Whilst this is due, in part, to the excellent levels of organic preservation and the spectacular range of artefacts, it also reflects the quality of the excavation and the ways in which Clark had brought together the different strands of data to create such a detailed picture of prehistoric life. The importance of Star Carr is also a testament to the role that Clark played in the development of Mesolithic archaeology and his enduring influence in the discipline.

The Vale of Pickering Research Trust

Following Clark's excavations, there was a break in research of this area for 25 years. It is not clear why this was, but perhaps researchers considered Star Carr to be a typical site for the period and hence further excavations may have been deemed unnecessary. In addition, Clark thought that he had excavated the full extent of Star Carr and thus there was little reason to do any further work at that particular location.

In 1976, work resumed in this landscape, undertaken by the Archaeology Division of the Department of Environment (now English Heritage) and North Yorkshire County Council. An area of 40 hectares of Seamer Carr Farm had been purchased for the development of a waste disposal and processing plant for Scarborough. The Seamer Carr project was headed up by Tim Schadla-Hall in order to look for sites in advance of construction work. Between 1975 and 1985, a programme of systematic sampling was undertaken and excavation was carried out on a number of sites dating from the Late Palaeolithic to the Iron Age. From the 1980s onwards the programme of test pitting, large-scale excavation and environmental sampling focused on the Early Mesolithic archaeology. Overall, nearly 2km of former lake shoreline was sampled, two large sites were excavated (Seamer Carr sites C and K), and a number of other more localised concentrations of materials discovered. In addition, further work was undertaken to understand the full extent of the lake and its ecological history.

Figure 3.8 *The excavations at Seamer Carr Site K in 1986*

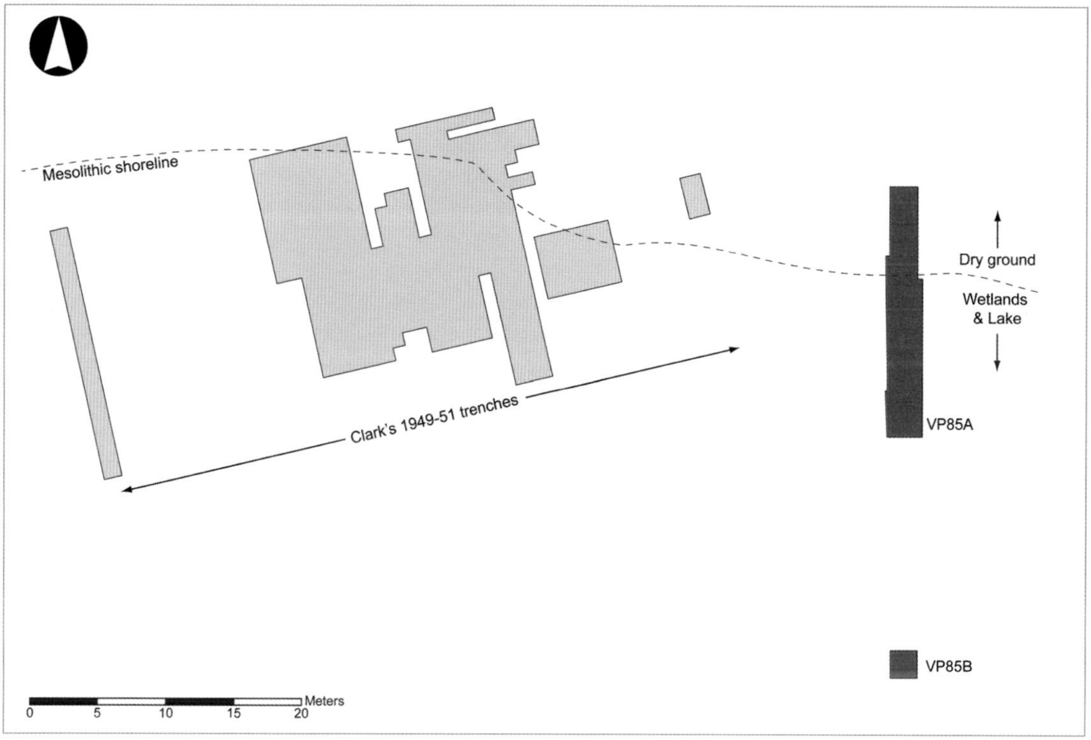
Mesolithic shoreline
Clark's 1949-51 trenches
Dry ground
Wetlands
& Lake
VP85A
VP85B
0
5
10
15
20
Meters

Figure 3.9 *The location of the two 1985 trenches in relation to Grahame Clark's excavations*

The Vale of Pickering Research Trust (VPRT) was set up in 1985 at the end of the Seamer Carr work, in order to continue the landscape-based investigation of the Early Mesolithic archaeology around Lake Flixton. The Trust was set up as a registered charity and is still in existence, administered by a board of Trustees comprising members of local businesses as well as professional archaeologists. The aims of the VPRT are to examine:

1. The entire shoreline of the palaeo-lake Flixton
2. Similar topographic locations to those identified at Seamer Carr
3. Known sites identified by John Moore
4. Potential new locations for Mesolithic archaeology

The first task that the Trust set itself was to establish a more precise record of the environments that had been present at Star Carr during the Mesolithic. To achieve this, a team led by Tim Schadla-Hall excavated two new trenches at the site in 1985 to collect samples for environmental analysis and radiocarbon dating. In order to avoid disturbing any archaeology that may have been missed by Clark, these new trenches were excavated almost 30m further along the former lake shore. Despite this, the Trust uncovered further evidence for Mesolithic activity, which would radically alter our understanding of the site.

Figure 3.10 *Plan of the timber platform discovered during the 1985 excavations at Star Carr*

As they excavated through the peat, the Trust's archaeologists began to find pieces of animal bone, antler, worked flints and even a barbed antler point. This provided the first indication that the site at Star Carr was far larger than Clark had thought. Then, towards the base of the trench they made a startling discovery as the remains of several substantial wooden timbers started to emerge. As the archaeologists continued to work it became clear that these were not isolated finds, but formed part of a large platform or trackway.

In 1989, the Trust re-excavated the trench and extended it slightly to allow more of the timbers to be exposed. Analysis carried out by Maisie Taylor, Britain's leading wood-working expert, showed that the timbers had been taken from much larger pieces of wood, either branches or entire tree trunks, which had been split by hammering wedges into them. By following the natural grain of the wood these large timbers could be broken down into progressively thinner pieces, which were then shaped by using a flint axe or adze. Once split, the sharp edges of the split wood appear to have been smoothed down further. We also have evidence that one timber had been split twice, making what we would term today a plank. Many of the others appear to have been split once and then most were laid down into the mud with their flat surface uppermost.

Seasonality studies and Star Carr

One of the most debated aspects of Clark's original interpretation of Star Carr was the time of year that the site was occupied, as this is a key question when considering hunter-gatherer communities. In the original analysis this was based on the annual growth cycle of red deer antler. Red deer carry their antlers between October and April, after which shed antler could be collected. By comparing this pattern with the material found at Star Carr, Clark concluded that the unshed antler could only have come from animals that were hunted during the winter and spring, whilst the natural shed material was collected in April. However, since the late 1970s a number of archaeologists have argued that this interpretation, and the data that it is based on, is wrong. Seamus Caulfield, for example, pointed out that antler had clearly been valued as a raw material and so may have been collected elsewhere and then brought to Star Carr; it thus didn't necessarily reflect the season of occupation of the site. Roger Jacobi noted that the unshed roe deer antler (which is not used as a raw material) pointed towards occupation into the early summer, rather than the winter and spring suggested by Clark.

In an attempt to understand the season of use better, Tony Legge and Peter Rowley-Conwy reanalysed the animal remains from Star Carr, but excluded the red deer skulls and antler. Instead, they looked at the time of year that the teeth of young animals begin to develop and used this to establish when the animals had been killed. They concluded that most had been hunted during the late spring and early summer, between April and May, and argued that this was when people would have been living at Star Carr. These estimates were refined through a more precise analysis of the tooth growth and eruption data collected by Richard Carter, which suggested that most of the young animals had been killed slightly earlier in the year.

Meanwhile, other researchers have also considered the seasonality question. Caroline Grigson noted that some of the birds that were found at Star Carr would have been present only in the summer, while Petra Dark has used botanical evidence to establish the season of occupation at Star Carr. By looking at the sorts of plant materials that had been burnt at the site, and assuming that the burning was caused by the actions of humans, she argued that people had been present at Star Carr for at least the summer months (late April to August).

But while these new analyses seem to suggest occupation in the summer months, the data from Clark's excavations are questionable because we now know that much of the animal bone recovered was not kept, which may have distorted the results. We also now know that the site is much larger than Clark thought, so butchery could have been carried out on different parts of the site, or indeed elsewhere in the landscape. The botanical evidence is also inconclusive as plants don't produce easily recognisable elements, such as seeds or buds, in the winter.

All in all there is no reason to suggest that Star Carr was only inhabited during a particular season, and it is possible that people were visiting the site repeatedly at different times of the year.

Not only was this the earliest evidence of carpentry ever discovered in Northern Europe, it also showed that the people living at Star Carr had a very sophisticated understanding of wood-working. Interestingly, some of the pieces of worked antler that Clark had recorded were the correct size and shape to have been used as wedges, so these may have been employed in the construction of the platform.

As well as these exciting new archaeological finds, the analysis of the environmental samples also led to some surprising and important discoveries. A detailed study of the microscopic pollen and fragments of charcoal within the peat carried out by Petra Dark showed that the reed beds at the edge of the lake had been cleared deliberately by fire over long periods of time. This was probably intended to open up the lake-edge area, making it easier for people arriving at the site by boat to reach the lake shore; it may also have been carried out to promote fresh plant growth. By dating the episodes of burning, using very precise radiocarbon dating, it was possible to establish a more accurate chronology for the occupation of the site. This showed that Star Carr was inhabited somewhere in the range of 9300–8400 BC and that people had intermittently revisited it over a period of around 300 years.

The work carried out by the VPRT began to improve our understanding of the site, but it also raised a number of new questions. First, whilst it was clear that Star Carr was larger than the area investigated by Clark, no one knew just how big an area it covered or what sorts of activities might have been carried out in other parts of the site. There was also the question of the timber platform: where did this go, and what was it used for?

However, it was not just these new excavations that were changing the way we thought about Star Carr. Since the late 1970s archaeologists had begun to reassess the evidence collected by Clark, leading to a number of different, and often contradictory, interpretations of the site. Some archaeologists argued that the animal bones indicated that the site was occupied during the summer months rather than the winter, and that it had been inhabited by small groups of hunters rather than entire families. Others suggested that the area excavated by Clark would have been underwater during the Mesolithic, and that artefacts had been thrown away as rubbish from a hitherto undiscovered settlement area. More recently, several archaeologists have argued that the artefacts recorded by Clark may have been deposited deliberately at the edge of the lake as a form of votive or ritual offering to ensure successful hunts.

These differing interpretations became the subject of intense debate, and without further excavation it was not possible to come to any agreement as to what the archaeology at Star Carr represented. Unfortunately, the work in the 1980s had shown that the peat was starting to dry out, and that it might not be long before the deposits, and all the archaeological material they contained, deteriorated to the point where they were no longer of any value.

Recent work

It was for this reason that a new team of archaeologists, led by Chantal Conneller, Nicky Milner and Barry Taylor, began working on the site in 2004. The first task was to create an accurate map of

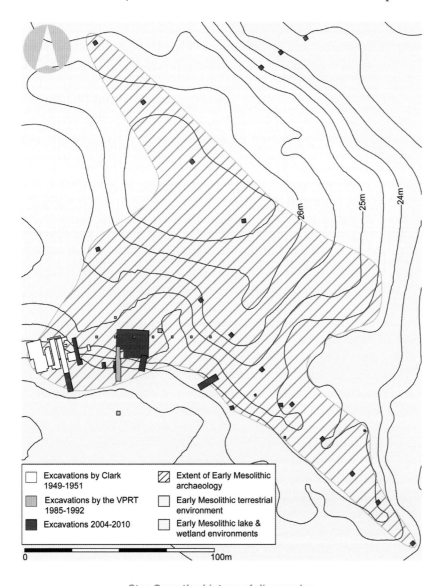

Figure 3.11 *The full extent of early Mesolithic activity at Star Carr*

26m   25m   24m

Excavations by Clark 1949-1951

Excavations by the VPRT 1985-1992

Excavations 2004-2010

Extent of Early Mesolithic archaeology

Early Mesolithic terrestrial environment

Early Mesolithic lake & wetland environments

0   100m

the buried Mesolithic landscape and then to use the plant and insect remains preserved in the peat to work out what plant communities would have been growing in the local area and hence where the lake shore would have been. Once the site had been mapped, fieldwalking surveys were carried out over what would have been the area of dry ground. This is a form of survey where archaeologists walk over cultivated fields systematically recording artefacts that have been brought up onto the modern ground surface in the course of ploughing. In addition, a number of small square trenches, known as test-pits, were excavated across the dry land area and several more were dug on higher ground further to the north. This work revealed that the site was much larger than ever imagined. Hundreds of worked flints were recorded by fieldwalking and dense scatters were present in almost all of the test-pits. In all, Mesolithic flint material covered an area approximately 20,000m², the equivalent of three full-sized football pitches.

Excavations were also undertaken in the waterlogged parts of the site, on what would have been the lake shore and the shallow waters just beyond it. The discoveries here have allowed the story of Star Carr to be developed further. To begin with, small quantities of animal bone, antler, and worked flint have been discovered in the peat that had formed at the edge of the lake. In some cases this material appears to have been thrown away as rubbish but in others the artefacts reflect activities that were being carried out in the wetlands. For example, in several of the trenches the flint includes large flakes and blades that have signs of damage along their cutting edge. These may have been used to cut reeds or other wetland plants, which were then used as food or as material for making artefacts such as mats or baskets. In another trench, a large piece of antler was found with a scatter of flints around it. This appears to be the waste from an episode of antler-working that was carried out at the margins of the lake-edge wetlands.

More information has also been revealed about the worked timber platform. Timbers have now been found in four trenches and, according to Maisie Taylor, most have been split and hewn in a similar manner to those recorded in 1985. While there are still large areas that need to be excavated, the distribution of the timbers in the trenches suggests that they form part of a larger structure, such as a series of platforms or system of trackways that extended for at least 30m along the shore. The timbers also ran into the area excavated by Clark and lay underneath the brushwood. Given the size of some of the timbers and the large area that they covered, the construction of the platforms must have been a considerable undertaking and would have required the collaborative effort of a large group of people.

Sadly for the archaeology, we also discovered that the site was no longer well preserved. The antler that was uncovered was very thin, leathery in texture, and in extremely poor condition. Although both Moore and Clark had found similarly badly preserved bone and antler, theirs had been found in the drier parts of the site: the more recent findings were in the supposedly waterlogged zones. With funding from English Heritage, further investigations were made which produced a number of disturbing results. The primary cause for concern was the extreme acidity of the sediments containing the archaeology: originally the peat must have had a near neutral pH allowing bone and antler to survive for thousands of years but in recent years the sediments had changed to a pH of below 3 in the archaeological zone, equivalent in strength to stomach acid. This acid strips away the mineral content of the bone, leaving the collagen, turning it into a 'jelly-bone': if you hold it between two fingers you can easily bend it like a piece of jelly. The reason for these changes is thought to be alterations to the water table caused by drainage. The lowering of the water table, to below the level of the archaeology, has allowed oxygen into the deposits, resulting in both the introduction of bacteria which eat the organic material, and chemical reactions taking place which have caused the increased acidity.

In two different years, the team re-excavated two of Clark's trenches. The first excavation was undertaken in order to study the level of degradation closer to the area where Clark had discovered well-preserved artefacts in the waterlogged levels. Although the preservation in this trench was fairly poor, part of the brushwood discovered by Clark still survived, as well as a handful of artefacts such as worked flint and antler-working waste. The second was a re-excavation of Clark's Cutting II, which was carried out to record the peat in greater detail and to take samples for environmental analysis. Remarkably the preservation in Cutting II was much better than elsewhere on site and the pH was a lot less acidic, possibly due to the way in which this trench had been backfilled at the end of the excavation in 1950. The birch tree originally found by Clark was also still lying in the trench although its end was missing. Presumably this had been sawn off and taken away for further analysis, although we have not discovered its current location.

Further work on this wood has shown that in contrast to the timber platforms the deposits of 'brushwood' have not been

Figure 3.12 *(a) The birch tree, showing its cut end, and (b) some of the animal bones that were found during the re-excavation of one of Grahame Clark's trenches in 2010*

Figure 3.13 *A broken barbed point discovered by Dr Amy Gray Jones during the re-excavation of Grahame Clark's trenches in 2010*

Discovery of pottery

During the re-excavation of one of Clark's trenches, the archaeologist Edward Blinkhorn found several pieces of pottery. This brought to mind an old tale which recounted that one of the students had planted some pottery on the site as a joke. The story goes that Clark had initially believed that it really was Mesolithic pottery and had even sent telegrams to Denmark to inform other scholars of this discovery, but that on finding out that it was fake, he was so angry he never returned to Star Carr again. Amazingly, we were able to find out the true story through the visit of the Hon. Robert Erskine who was visiting the site as a guest of Richard Marriott (the Chair of the Vale of Pickering Research Trust). It turned out that not only had

Figure 3.14 *The Honourable Robert Erskine (far left) and Dr Ed Blinkhorn (left), with Professor Nicky Milner (right) and Mr Richard Marriott (far right)*

Robert been digging on site when the pottery was found, but it was he who had found it: he told us that one of the other students had planted it in his square and when he found it he took it to Clark. Clark later came out to the trench with it and asked whether it was a joke, and when they admitted to it, he took it in good humour!

worked using axes. We now know that the brushwood was mainly composed of willow and/or aspen stems, some of which may have fallen from trees growing by the shore. However, it is possible that some of this wood may have been deposited here by people, perhaps again to stabilise the peat.

What was also intriguing was that there were pieces of bone in the soil that the archaeologists in the 1950s had thrown back into the trench (known as 'backfill'), including large numbers of rib bones: it has since been confirmed by people who worked on the site that Clark did throw away a lot of bone which could not be identified to a particular animal species.

As well as re-excavating Clark's trenches, large-scale excavations also took place on the dry land just above the lake

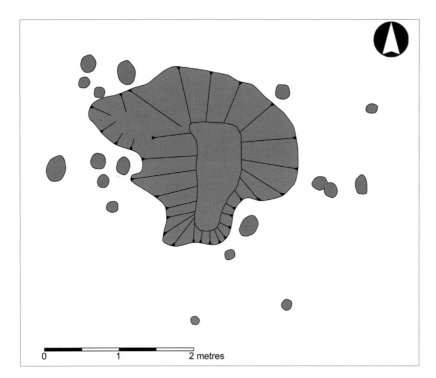

0   1   2 metres

shore, an area that had never been investigated in great detail in the past. To begin with, these excavations revealed dense scatters of worked flint and smaller quantities of very crumbly animal bone but as work continued a new and altogether unexpected discovery was made. As the layers of sediments were carefully excavated, a large area of much darker material was gradually uncovered, several metres wide, with a series of smaller oval patches around it. This area was also much richer in finds than the other parts of the trench, and nearly every scrape of the trowel seemed to produce another piece of flint.

Excavating this darker material revealed a large, deliberately dug hollow, surrounded by a series of smaller, round holes that had originally held posts. This was clearly the remains of a 'house', similar to the one discovered at Howick. However, the Star Carr structure is substantially earlier, dating to around 9000 BC, making it the oldest 'house' in the country.

It is difficult to know exactly how the house was built because the remains are very slight. We presume that the centre, where there was a hollow, was scooped out and then around the edge a number of holes were dug for posts. In a period before spades were invented, people would have had to use mattocks and/or digging sticks or antlers to break up the sod and create the hollows and postholes. There are no surviving building materials from the structure itself but we think that timbers would have been placed in the postholes to create a roughly circular shape and then lashed together in some way. Although we haven't found any such evidence, it is possible that people made twine out of plant materials such as nettles which are known to produce good fibres for string-making; we know from the pollen records that these grew at the site. It is also impossible to know what people used for covering the house, but it may have been animal hides or, perhaps more likely, reeds which grew in abundance only metres away. These could have been chopped down with sharp pieces of flint and used for thatching, much as is done today in some parts of Britain for roofing on traditional timber-framed buildings, making the structure waterproof.

Analysis of the sediments from within the hollow have shown that it contained large quantities of organic material: this may be the result of people laying down reeds or other plants as flooring. It is very difficult to be sure how long the house was in use. At some sites, such as Howick, radiocarbon dating has shown that structures were in use for several generations. Unfortunately there is no material suitable for radiocarbon dating in the Star Carr house, but the positioning of some of the postholes suggests at least one phase of rebuilding.

A small scatter of burnt flint found within the hollow may

have been caused by a small fire or hearth that was used to light or heat the structure. Similar scatters found outside of the structure were probably created by camp fires. We haven't found the remains of any hearths but this may simply be because they don't survive in the archaeological record. If hearths are dug into the ground, or lined with stones, they are easier to identify archaeologically, but if they are simply constructed of firewood which burns right down there is little evidence remaining once the fire has burnt out, any remaining charcoal and ash being gradually dispersed by the wind and rain.

Conclusion

Since its discovery in 1948, the excavations at Star Carr have provided archaeologists with a wealth of information about life in the Mesolithic. From the spectacular artefacts made from bone and antler that were discovered by Clark to the more recent discoveries of the timber platforms and the house, these finds have transformed our understanding of the early prehistoric hunter-gatherer communities who lived in Britain in the centuries following the end of the last Ice Age. Before we go on to look at how we can interpret this information, we must first look at how work in the surrounding area has built up a picture of the landscape around Star Carr.

Figure 3.16 *Part of the timber platform uncovered during excavations at Star Carr in 2010*

Suggested further reading

For detailed information about the site, the best places to start are the reports on Clark's excavations and the subsequent work of the Vale of Pickering Research Trust.

Excavations at Star Carr. An early Mesolithic site at Seamer near Scarborough, Yorkshire, by Grahame Clark

Star Carr in Context, by Paul Mellars and Petra Dark

The various debates surrounding the reinterpretation of the site are summarised in the following articles, all of which include references to the original publications.

'A History of Environmental Archaeology at Star Carr', by Barry Taylor (in *Encyclopaedia of Global Archaeology*)

Star Carr Revisited: A Re-analysis of the Large Mammals, by Anthony Legge and Peter Rowley-Conwy

'Star Carr reanalysed', by Richard Chatterton, and 'Star Carr recontextualised', by Chantal Conneller (both published in *Peopling the Mesolithic in a northern environment*, edited by Jenny Moore and Lynne Bevan)

Several accounts of the recent excavations at Star Carr have been published in *British Archaeology*.

'Fading Star', by Nicky Milner (*British Archaeology* **96**)

'Little House by the Shore', by Barry Taylor, Chantal Conneller and Nicky Milner (*British Archaeology* **115**)

More technical accounts can be found in the following publications:

'Substantial settlement in the European early Mesolithic: new research at Star Carr', by Chantal Conneller, Nicky Milner, Barry Taylor and Masie Taylor (*Antiquity* **86**)

'Star Carr in the new millennium', by Chantal Conneller, Nicky Milner, Tim Schadla-Hall, and Barry Taylor (published in *From Bann flakes to Bushmills. Papers in honour of Professor Peter Woodman*, edited by Nyree Finlay, Sinead McCartan, Nicky Milner and Caroline Wickham-Jones)

The Star Carr landscape

4

Introduction

Since the mid-1940s, large-scale programmes of archaeological excavation and survey have been carried out in the area around Lake Flixton. As we have seen, this began with the work of John Moore, who carried out the first investigations of the lake and identified ten areas of human activity at sites around its shore. Over the past 35 years, further work has been carried out by the Vale of Pickering Research Trust. As well as mapping much of the former lake edge, the Trust has discovered more than ten additional sites, many of which were contemporary with Star Carr, and has developed a detailed record of the changing nature of this landscape. This chapter explains how the lake has been mapped, the process of discovery for other sites and how we can reconstruct the environment from the plant remains which have been preserved in the peat.

Mapping the hidden landscape

Methods

One of the biggest problems facing archaeologists who work in this area is that both the lake and the surrounding landscape are buried beneath thick deposits of peat. In order to record this hidden landscape, archaeologists have taken hundreds of detailed measurements of the depth of the peat that formed across it. This is done using a device called an auger, which is

Figure 4.1 *Archaeologists from the Vale of Pickering Research Trust carrying out an auger survey*

pushed down into the peat and extracts a thin section of sediment which can then be examined and recorded in the field. By taking these measurements at regular intervals and then surveying the modern ground surface it is possible to map the topography of the land-surface beneath the peat. Once this has been done, data from the plant remains preserved in the peat can then be used to calculate the level of the lake and the location of the main plant communities, creating a map of the landscape as it was 11,000 years ago.

Our evidence for the environments that formed across this landscape comes, for the most part, from material that has been preserved within the lake itself. To begin with, the sediments that built up within the lake reflect the nature of the environment in which they formed. Sediments that built up in deep water, for example, generally consist of very fine-grained organic sediment whilst those forming in shallower conditions often contain a larger proportion of plant material because more plants, such as reeds, were growing in this part of the lake. Furthermore, as the sediments began to accumulate they trapped and preserved the remains of the plants, insects and other small animals that were growing and living in the surrounding area. Since these are suited to particular ecological factors, such as temperature, water depth,

Figure 4.2 *Layers of sand and peat from the bottom of the lake sampled in an auger*

Figure 4.3 *Students from the University of Manchester working on the excavations at Flixton School House Farm on the southern edge of Lake Flixton*

and shade, we can reconstruct the environmental conditions by looking at the species that are present. What is more, by looking at how the types of plants or insects change in different layers of sediments we can see how the environment developed over time.

As well as mapping this physical landscape, archaeologists have also been recording the evidence for the people who lived around the lake during the Mesolithic. To do this they have excavated several hundred small trenches at regular intervals along the edge of the Mesolithic lake shore. Where archaeological material, such as worked flint or animal bone, has been discovered, more trenches have been excavated in order to establish the size of the site and to get a better idea of the sorts of activities that were taking place there. Using this approach, new sites have been discovered and several of the sites first identified by John Moore have been studied in more detail.

These excavations and surveys are a collaborative process, involving a team of archaeologists, each with their own particular skills and specialisms. Experienced field archaeologists carry out the excavation itself, whilst a surveyor maps the location of the

The Star Carr landscape

trench and each individual artefact found within it. Specialists in the study of Mesolithic flint tools and animal bone identify and record the artefacts as they are discovered, and environmental archaeologists make detailed studies of the peat in order to understand the type of environment that the objects were deposited into. University students and members of the local community also take part in the fieldwork, where they learn the techniques of excavation and survey. In some cases these students become specialists in their own right, and eventually lead their own research projects on sites across the world.

Macrofossils have been used in conjunction with the analysis of pollen and spores to produce very detailed records of the changing environments around the lake. At several sites, pollen analysis was used to reconstruct the plant communities growing on the island, whilst the macrofossils provided a very precise account of the changing character of the wetlands that were developing at the shore. As they reflect the composition of the local environment, macrofossils have also been used to establish the nature of the environments into which archaeological material had been deposited.

Interpreting the evidence

Drawing the different strands of data together it has been possible to reconstruct the environmental history of the lake and the surrounding landscape. The origin of the lake dates back to the height of the last Ice Age, when much of Britain was covered by glaciers. One of these, known as the North Sea ice sheet, advanced into the Vale of Pickering, extending almost as far as the modern village of Staxton, whilst another moved south across the Vale of York. With both ends of the Vale of Pickering blocked by these massive glaciers, water draining from the Moors and Wolds became trapped, and a large lake formed within the valley. This is known as the Glacial Lake Pickering. As the climate began to improve, the glaciers slowly melted, and Lake Pickering disappeared. However, the retreating ice left an undulating landscape of large shallow hollows, low hills and ridges across the valley floor. Water from the surrounding area drained into the largest of these hollows creating Lake Flixton, whilst the hills and ridges became islands and peninsulas. As temperatures rose, wetland plants quickly colonised the lake, whilst grasses, shrubs and eventually birch and pine trees became established across the surrounding landscape.

Reconstructing past environments

The plant remains that are preserved in lake and wetland sediments, such as peat, can provide a wealth of information about what the environment was like in the past. By looking at the sorts of plants that are present in a layer of peat, for example, we can tell what species were growing in the surrounding area, how deep the lake was, and what the climate was like. We can also see how the environment changed over time by looking at the plant remains from different layers of sediment.

Perhaps the most important and widely used form of plant remains are microscopic pollen and spores, a class of material that is known collectively as microfossils. These are produced in large quantities by most species of plant, and can be dispersed over relatively long distances, either by wind or water, or through the actions of insects and other animals. As such they provide a record of the vegetation that was growing around the site as well as in the wider landscape. However, the interpretation of microfossils

is quite complex and requires a good understanding of the plants themselves as well as the environments into which the pollen and spores were being deposited.

One of the most significant issues that has to be addressed is distinguishing between the plants that were present in the local area and those that were growing in the wider landscape. Some trees produce pollen that can travel for tens (or sometimes hundreds) of kilometres, whilst any streams that ran into the lake could carry pollen from plants growing in the surrounding landscape. This material becomes mixed with the pollen and spores from plants growing around the shore before becoming incorporated with the sediments forming within the lake. As such, the analysis of the pollen from these sediments will provide a record of the regional vegetation but without any indication of the spatial distribution of the particular plant communities.

However, where deposits were forming in areas of very dense vegetation, such as in reedswamps or woodlands, the plants

Figure 4.4 *Collecting samples of wood from Mesolithic peat deposits in the former Lake Flixton. Analysis of the wood can determine the species of tree that it came from, helping archaeologists to reconstruct the character of the local vegetation*

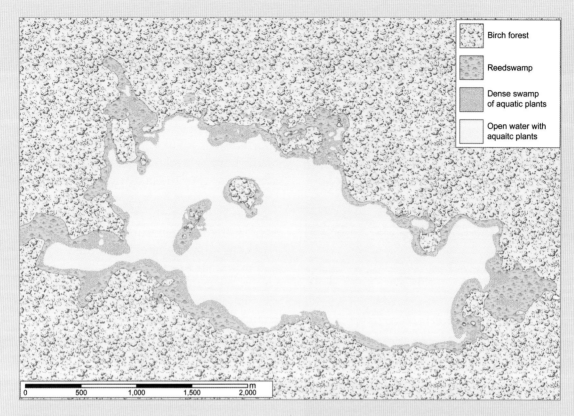

Figure 4.5 *Map showing Lake Flixton at the start of the early Mesolithic and the environments that were forming around it*

growing in the local area will deposit a far higher proportion of microfossils in to the peat than the plants growing further away. By looking at the pollen and spores from these sediments it is possible to produce a very accurate record of the vegetation that was growing at that particular location. What is more, by recording the pollen and spores from different parts of a site it is possible to map the distribution of the principal environments at particular points in time.

This approach has been adopted at several sites around Lake Flixton, helping us to understand how the environments within the lake gradually developed. In the north-west of the lake, at Seamer Carr, Ed Cloutman analysed the pollen from eight separate locations, and used the results to map the main areas of wetland and terrestrial vegetation at different stages during the Mesolithic. Similar techniques were used at Star Carr and showed that the reedswamp that was growing along the shore was gradually replaced by fen and carr environments during the course of the Early Mesolithic.

The larger plant remains are known as macrofossils; these include nuts, seeds and fruits, as well as stems, leaves and branches. Unlike microfossils these do not travel over such long distances and provide a more accurate picture of the local patterns of vegetation. Some macrofossils can also be identified to a higher taxonomic level than pollen, and provide a more precise record of the plants that were present at particular locations.

The development of plant life within and around the lake was interrupted by the return to cold conditions during the Younger Dryas. Many of the species that had been growing in the area were unsuited to the much colder climate and died out, leaving a more open landscape covered with grasses and shrubs. Some of the hardier wetland plants may have survived within the lake, though the water levels would have been much lower and the lake is likely to have frozen during the winter when temperatures fell.

As the climate improved at the very end of the Ice Age (c 9600 cal BC) plants became re-established in the area and the character of the landscape began to change. To begin with pioneer species, such as bur-reed and bulrush, recolonised the lake whilst scrub vegetation, including juniper and willow, became established across the areas of grassland. Within a few hundred years, however, dense beds of reeds and sedges had formed around the edge of the lake, whilst aquatic plants thrived in the deeper water. At the shore, willow and aspen were growing on the damp waterlogged soil, and a forest of birch and pine, interspersed with open grassland, covered the areas of higher ground beyond the lake.

We know from research carried out at sites around the lake that these environments would have been very diverse. The differences in the depths of water around the lake would have meant that whilst in some areas there would

Figure 4.6 The different types of environment that were forming around the edge of the lake during the early Mesolithic: (a) reedswamp in shallow water; (b) willow and reeds at the water's edge;
(c) trees growing directly over the peat that has formed at the edge of the lake

have been dense beds of reeds, in others there would have been a thin fringe of vegetation along the shore. The composition of the wetland vegetation was also very diverse, with a range of aquatic and emergent plants growing amongst the reeds as well as in the deeper waters further from the shore. A variety of different shrubs and herbaceous plants grew across the dry ground, and there is evidence for small-scale clearings within the woodland.

It was within this environment that the inhabitants of the Mesolithic sites around the lake lived. At most of these sites, large, dense scatters of worked flint have been recorded from what would have been the dry ground just above the lake shore, along with smaller quantities of animal bone and, more occasionally, features such as hearths, pits or arrangements of postholes. Analysis of the worked flint has shown that these 'scatters' are often the result of numerous episodes of activity, carried out at different times and varying in both nature and scale. In some cases this involved the manufacture of particular tools, whilst in others the tools themselves were used, repaired, and then discarded. At some sites concentrations of burnt flint have been recorded within these scatters, probably evidence for the presence of a fire, around which people were working.

Features such as pits and postholes, which are numerous on later prehistoric sites, are very rare on Mesolithic sites but have been recorded at several locations around the lake. At Flixton School House Farm, on the southern shore of the lake, excavations recorded a concentration of over 35 small pits and postholes, most of which were clustered around a large, central feature, almost a metre deep. This may have acted as a cooking pit, as a scatter of large, heat-shattered stone was found a few metres away. Several of the features appear to have formed small structures, whilst some of the small pits appear to have been dug as part of an offering, possibly to commemorate the events taking place at the site.

Much smaller quantities of material have been recorded from the peat that formed around the edge of the lake. Here the collections include pieces of worked flint, fragments of animal bone, and pieces of antler. Unlike the material from the dry ground none of the flint appears to have been waste from tool manufacture, but instead reflects the use of sharp flint flakes and blades and other tools in tasks which were carried out within the lake-edge wetlands. These may have been lost or thrown away after tasks such as the cutting and collecting of reeds or other plants, or in the butchering of animals.

At several sites, the analysis of the pollen and microscopic

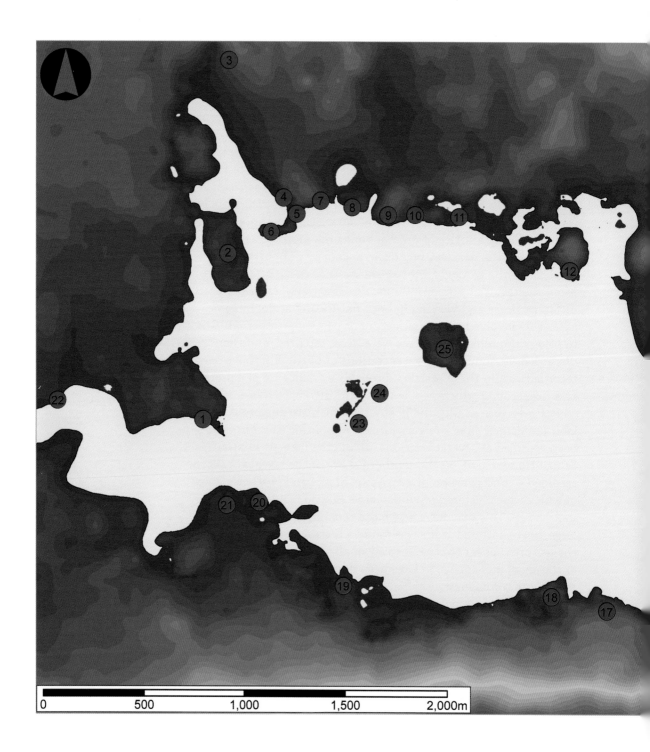

Figure 4.7 *All the known areas of Mesolithic activity that have been discovered around Lake Flixton*

Key: 1, Star Carr; 2, Ling Lane; 3, Seamer Carr Site F; 4, Seamer Carr Sites L and N; 5, Seamer Carr Site K; 6, Seamer Carr Site D; 7, Seamer Carr Site B (Rabbit Hill); 8, Seamer Carr Site C; 9, Manham Hill; 10–12, Cayton Carr; 13, Lingholme Site B; 14, Killerby Carr; 15, Lingholme Site A; 16, Barry's Island; 17, Flixton School Field; 18, Flixton School House Farm; 19, Woodhouse Farm; 20, VP Site E; 21, VP Site D; 22, Flixton Site 9; 23, Flixton Island Site 1; 24, Flixton Island Site 2; 25, No Name Hill

Figure 4.8 *A small pit filled with charcoal and burnt hazelnut shells and covered with stones, discovered during excavations at Flixton School House Farm in 2008. Scale unit 1cm*

charcoal preserved in the peat has shown that people were deliberately burning the lake-edge vegetation, often on successive occasions. This may have been carried out to remove any invasive plants and improve the quality of the reed and sedge beds, which would have provided a reliable source of raw materials.

These new sites reveal the variety of activities that were undertaken in different parts of the landscape around Lake Flixton. At Seamer C people were making tools for scraping hide and using them to process animal skins. They also brought in some of the meaty bones from an aurochs, which they had killed and butchered elsewhere. At Seamer K, activities were more varied and the place was probably revisited several times. On one occasion, people were focused on the intensive production of microliths – used as the tips and barbs of arrows; presumably they were gearing up for a hunting trip. At another site, Seamer B, people killed and butchered an aurochs. Several caches of flint nodules have also been found: people were storing flint, obtained several kilometres away, for future use.

As well as using the sites around the shore, we know that Mesolithic people visited the two islands in the lake, suggesting they regularly used boats to move over the waters of the lake. The smaller of the islands (Flixton Island) consists of two small hills, no more than 1.5m above the surface of the lake, which were connected by a narrow causeway. Evidence for Mesolithic activity on the island was first recorded by John Moore, who excavated a trench across the most southerly hill (Site 1) and recorded a dense scatter of worked flint, pieces of animal bone and antler, and the remains of hearths. Moore interpreted this as a camp that had been occupied by Mesolithic hunters. However, excavations at the site by the Vale of Pickering Research Trust have shown that activity was far more extensive than Moore had found and the island had probably been revisited on numerous occasions.

The second, larger island is known as 'No Name Hill', and it lies just a few hundred metres north of Flixton Island. This site was also discovered by John Moore but has been more thoroughly excavated by the Vale of Pickering Research Trust. This work recorded dense scatters of Mesolithic flint across the top of the island and smaller quantities of flint tools, animal bone, and fragments of red deer antler that had been deposited in the peat at the island's shore. By analysing this material, we have been able to identify some of the activities that people were carrying out on the island. This included sharpening axes, possibly to cut down trees or work large pieces of wood, manufacturing barbed points from pieces of red deer antler, and butchering and processing the carcasses of animals. People were also carrying out tasks within the swamp that involved using sharp flint blades, possibly to cut and collect wetland plants. As with other sites around the lake, people returned to No Name Hill on many occasions.

When this research started it was expected that more sites like Star Carr would be discovered, since archaeologists believed that Star Carr was typical of what a well-preserved Mesolithic site would look like. However, the evidence from these other sites around Lake Flixton suggests that this is not the case – many of the artefacts found at Star Carr in large numbers, such as the antler frontlets and beads, are absent at these other sites. Furthermore, while hearths and pits have been found, no hut structures or worked timbers have been found. The question remains: is Star Carr unique, or are there more sites like it that remain buried beneath the peat?

A changing landscape through the Mesolithic

Based on the analysis of the plant remains from sites around the lake we know that the character of the landscape changed throughout the time that sites such as Star Carr were occupied. Within the lake, the gradual accumulation of sediments caused the depth of water to become shallower, allowing beds of reeds and communities of aquatic plants to expand further from the shore. As this process continued, the deposits around the edge of the lake began to form above the level of the water and were colonised by trees and fen plants, whilst the areas of standing water gradually receded. The build-up of organic sediments also caused the ground around the edge of the lake to become more waterlogged and peat-forming wetlands began to expand over the previously dry ground beyond the shore.

The composition of the woodland surrounding the lake also changed as new species became established in the area. At around 8000 cal BC hazel became the main component of the woodland, whilst oak and elm were also starting to grow at sites in the area. Within approximately 1000 years these species had become more established and, along with ash and lime, formed mixed deciduous woodland that covered the surrounding dry ground.

Despite the profound changes to the nature of the landscape we know that people continued to inhabit this area throughout the Mesolithic. During the excavations at Seamer Carr a small assemblage of microliths was discovered in the peat that had formed over the Early Mesolithic land surface. These were arranged in two parallel lines and are thought to have been part of a composite tool, possibly an arrow that was lost or discarded within the wetlands. This dates to around 1000 years after the occupation of Star Carr. Radiocarbon dates on fragments of charcoal at Flixton School House Farm have shown that this site was also occupied at around the same time, and other Late Mesolithic sites have been identified on the basis of changes in flint tool technology.

The landscape that these people lived in would have been unrecognisable to the earlier inhabitants of this area. The area around the lake shore had become buried beneath the wetland deposits, and extensive areas of fen now separated the dry land from the remaining areas of open water. Some of the small hilly peninsulas, cut off by the expansion of the peat-forming environments, became small islands surrounded by wetlands, while the low-lying Flixton Island would have disappeared entirely. It is difficult to tell how conscious people would have been of the changes that were taking place, but it is possible that knowledge of the earlier landscape may have been passed on through stories. It is also very likely that some traces of the earlier inhabitants may still have been visible, such as the butchered bones of animals or old flint tools.

By around 6500 BC, the lake had changed beyond recognition. All but the deepest parts of the lake had been colonised by wetland plants, while areas of open water were reduced to a series of small pools connected by streams that cut through the surrounding swamps. The shallower parts of the lake and many of the embayments had become entirely infilled with peat and were covered by trees and fen plants, and all that remained of the earlier hills and peninsulas were small islands in the ever-expanding swamp and fen.

Conclusion

At the start of the Mesolithic, Lake Flixton was a large but relatively shallow body of water, almost 4km across and nearly 8m deep in places. There were two islands within the lake, which have been named 'Flixton Island' and 'No Name Hill', and a series of low hilly peninsulas and large, deep embayments along the shore. Wetland vegetation thrived in the shallow waters of the lake, providing habitats for birds and animals, and a woodland of birch and pine trees covered large parts of the surrounding landscape. By the end of the Mesolithic, however, the lake had disappeared, and an environment of swamps and fens interspersed with small streams and shallow pools of water had formed in its place. Wetland environments had also formed across areas of previously dry ground beyond the lake shores, and the birch forest had been replaced by mixed woodland of deciduous trees such as oak, elm and ash.

Recording and mapping these changing environments is crucial to our understanding of the human occupation of this landscape. The different plant communities would have been a source of food and raw materials as well as providing the habitats for the animals that people hunted. As such, the tasks and activities that people undertook would have varied at different locations around the lake depending upon the presence and abundance of particular species of plants and the character of the local environment. What is more, the patterns of human activity would have changed over time as the environments within the lake and the surrounding area developed. Resources that were available to people at the start of the Mesolithic may have been scarce by the end of the period, whilst the habitats of particular animals may have shifted to other parts of the landscape. At the same time, the arrival of new plant species would have meant that people had access to different foods and raw materials.

The search for the Mesolithic can be like looking for a needle in a haystack, but the concerted efforts of John Moore and the archaeologists working for the Vale of Pickering Research Trust have provided one of the most detailed pictures ever of a populated Mesolithic landscape. However, there are still questions which remain to be solved. For instance, what did people do with their dead in this area: have we missed the cemeteries, or did they perhaps cremate the dead and scatter their ashes? Why have we not found any boats? And why have we not found any other sites like Star Carr? Lake Flixton clearly still has much that it can tell us about the Mesolithic, and only by carrying out more research can we hope to unlock its secrets.

Suggested further reading

John Moore's work was first published in the *Proceedings of the Prehistoric Society* in 1950 and as an appendix in Grahame Clark's publication of the Star Carr excavations.

The work of the Vale of Pickering Research Trust will be published in the next few years, but the following articles summarise the work that has taken place and what it means for our understanding of the Mesolithic occupation of this landscape.

'Beyond Star Carr: The Vale of Pickering in the Tenth Millennium BP', by Chantal Conneller, and Tim Schadla-Hall (*Proceedings of the Prehistoric Society* **69**)

'Inhabiting new landscapes: Settlement and mobility in Britain after the last glacial maximum', by Chantal Conneller (*Oxford Journal of Archaeology* **26**:3)

'Star Carr in a Postglacial Lakescape: 60 years of Research', by Nicky Milner, Paul Lane, Barry Taylor, Chantal Conneller and Tim Schadla-Hall (*Journal of Wetland Archaeology* **11**)

'Early Mesolithic activity in the wetlands of the Lake Flixton Basin', by Barry Taylor (*Journal of Wetland Archaeology* **11**)

Reconstructing life at Star Carr 11,000 years ago

5

Introduction

Since it was first discovered over 60 years ago, Star Carr has formed the basis for many of our interpretations of life in the Mesolithic. As further discoveries have been made, either through excavation or through the application of new scientific techniques, old interpretations have been challenged and new ideas have developed, allowing archaeologists to create an even more detailed picture of life at the site.

In some cases this new work has challenged and even contradicted Clark's original ideas about the site. When Clark excavated Star Carr, he saw it as the temporary camp of a small group of hunter-gatherers, who moved from place to place as they followed migrating herds of animals. This view of early Mesolithic society as consisting of small, highly mobile groups has remained popular amongst many archaeologists, but it is a view that our current work at Star Carr has called into question. The sheer size of the site and the length of time during which it was occupied or revisited are at odds with the idea of small groups of hunter-gatherers, whilst the house and the timber platforms suggest a more settled way of life. Furthermore, such constructions would have involved the cooperation of a large number of people, with different skills and abilities. Trees had to be felled, the wood worked into timbers, and the reedswamp cleared before the heavy planks were moved into place. This implies a relatively large number of people, who were willing to invest their time and labour in one particular place.

Whilst some of Clark's interpretations have been disproved by our more recent discoveries, his work continues to provide an important foundation for our current understanding of the site. The spectacular assemblage of artefacts, for example, remains the most important source of information that we have for bone- and antler-working technology in the Mesolithic. What is more, it was Clark who began the tradition of well-integrated archaeological and environmental studies that form the basis for the way we excavate wetland sites today. Thus, the following account of life at Star Carr owes as much to the work carried out by Clark and his team as it does to the current generation of archaeologists working at the site.

Life at Star Carr, 9000 BC

When people first arrived at Star Carr, over 11,000 years ago, the site lay on the southern shore of a large peninsula on the western side of the lake. There were two small hills at the north of the site and a long spit of land to the east, which formed a narrow promontory extending into the lake. Birch trees and ferns were growing across much of the peninsula, and willow and aspen trees were present along the shore. Dense beds of reeds and sedges were established in the shallow waters at the edge of the lake, whilst water-lilies and other aquatic plants flourished in the deeper water.

These first visitors to Star Carr established a camp within the birch forest, close to the water's edge. Although we don't know how many people arrived at this time, or how long they stayed, we do know that the site continued to be inhabited for the following 200–300 years. We also know from the recent excavations that the dry ground above the lake shore formed the main living area, and that it was here that people carried out many of their day-to-day tasks. Analysis of the thousands of pieces of worked flint that were recorded from this area has shown that people were manufacturing a wide range of different tools. Some of these were taken away to be used at other locations, whilst others were used, repaired and then discarded at Star Carr. Analysis of microscopic traces left on the flint has shown that these tools were used for a range of different tasks, including wood- and antler-working, and hide processing. It is very likely that some of the flint flakes and blades were also employed for cutting and working plant materials and for butchering animals, whilst others would have been taken away and used for hunting.

As well as working with flint, the inhabitants of Star Carr were also manufacturing tools and other objects from bone, antler and wood. Red deer antler in particular was being worked in a variety of different ways to produce numerous objects including barbed points, axes and mattocks. Although only a small number of wooden artefacts have been discovered at the site, we know that many more wooden objects would have been used by the people living at Star Carr. As Clark himself pointed out, many of the bone and antler objects would have had wooden handles or hafts, and these were probably manufactured at the site.

The circular 'structure' was built on the dry ground, about 5m from the water's edge. At present, it is difficult to say what its function was. Whilst it is tempting to call it a house because the natural assumption is that people used it for habitation and shelter, it is possible that it was used for something other than as a place to live and sleep. Some more recent hunter-gatherer groups in Patagonia (South America) lived in very flimsy shelters and only built substantial structures for ritual ceremonies, so we cannot rule out the possibility that the structure at Star Carr served a similar function.

What we do know is that people were making and using flint tools in the structure because large quantities of worked flint were discovered amongst the sediments that formed within it. These included burins, tools associated with antler-working, so it is possible that objects made from antler were also being manufactured here. However, this raises the question of how people could live in the structure when there was so much sharp flint on the floor. One possibility is that this large quantity of flint accumulated very slowly over time as pieces of flint were trodden into the floor. Alternatively, perhaps the assemblage represents the final phase of activity: on previous occasions, people may have cleaned the floor regularly, sweeping the flint outside.

Whilst many practical activities such as wood- or flint-working were carried out on the dry ground part of the site, we also know that people were carrying out tasks within the adjacent wetlands. In several of the excavations small quantities of flint flakes, blades, and other tools have been found within the peat at the lake edge. Analysis of these sediments shows that the artefacts were deposited into an area of shallow standing water where reeds and sedges were growing, and were probably lost or discarded whilst gathering wetland plants. Unfortunately there is no

Figure 5.1
(overleaf) Artist's reconstruction of the site at Star Carr (Dominic Andrews)

evidence for the use of these plants, but, as discussed in Chapter 2, data collected on other Mesolithic sites show that people were manufacturing a range of objects from plant materials. We also know that many of the plants growing at Star Carr were edible and there is evidence from other Mesolithic sites that people were preparing these, or similar species, to eat.

Although the manufacture of the barbed points may have taken place at different parts of the site, we know that at least part of the production process took place at the water's edge. The excavations carried out in the 1990s recorded a small concentration of flint burins close to the lake shore and pieces of antler-working waste were discovered in the adjacent swamp deposits. We know from experimental work that antler needs to be soaked in water before it can be worked and that it needs to be wetted frequently whilst the grooves are being cut and the splinter is being extracted. It seems very likely then that this stage of the barbed point production was taking place at the lake shore, the unfinished points then being taken away and completed elsewhere on the site.

Further evidence that people were carrying out tasks within the wetlands comes from the timber platforms. Based on environmental analysis we now know that these were constructed shortly after the site was first occupied, when the water at the edge of the lake was becoming shallower and ground conditions more boggy. As there are very few artefacts associated with the timbers they do not appear to have acted as occupation areas. Instead we think they were designed to make movement though the wetlands easier at a time when the build-up of peat had made the lake edge much boggier. They might have been for walking over as trackways but they may also have been used as slipways for boats.

As well as the day-to-day tasks that people were carrying out, there is also evidence for more ritualised forms of activity at Star Carr. This comes from a reanalysis of the bone and antler objects that were discovered by Clark, along with new studies of the plant remains from the peat where the objects were found. This new work suggests the bone and antler artefacts were not simply lost or thrown away, but were deliberately deposited into the swamp that was forming in the shallow water at the edge of the lake.

What is most intriguing is that although we have evidence for activity across the whole of the Star Carr peninsula, the bone and antler objects have only been found in a very small part of the site. What is more, when we look at these artefacts in detail it appears that they were deposited in a very deliberate manner. For example, although many of the objects, such as the barbed points and axes, would have been attached to wooden handles or hafts, only one of these was found when Clark excavated the site, and this was only a small broken and burnt section of handle. As wood survives in peat, it appears that the hafts and handles were deliberately removed before the objects were thrown into the lake. We can also see that whilst some of the objects were broken, many of the others were intact or could have been easily repaired and used again. Finally, whilst the objects had different functions, all of these tools were made from bone and antler, which suggests that people were deliberately selecting them on the basis of the materials they were manufactured from. When we consider all this evidence, it seems unlikely that the objects were being thrown away simply on a casual basis, but were being deliberately deposited.

However, whilst we can suggest that these objects were intentionally deposited into the lake-edge swamp, the motivations behind these acts are harder to deduce. One current theory is that they reflect culturally appropriate ways of disposing of objects that are made from the remains of animals. We know from anthropological studies that many hunter-gatherers understand animals very differently from us. Rather than being simply a food resource, or even pets, animals can be seen as friends, ancestors or spirits, and are often regarded as having souls and behaving, whilst among themselves, very like humans. Amongst these societies there are often very strict rules regarding the way the remains of animals are disposed of, and breaking these rules can result in bad luck and unsuccessful hunts.

Some archaeologists have suggested that the red deer antler frontlets may have been worn by shamans. In many societies shamans are ritual specialists and one of their tasks, indeed the act that most demonstrates their powers, is the ability to transform into animals in order to communicate with animal spirits. It is possible that the Star Carr antler frontlets, which when they were worn may have also had the skins attached, were powerful objects used by shamans during their 'transformation' into animals. If this is the case, it appears that red deer were the animal deemed to be most spiritually important to the people that inhabited Star Carr.

While Star Carr may have formed the focus for many aspects of people's lives, some activities, such as hunting, took place away from the site and would have involved journeys into the surrounding landscape. Some of these journeys almost certainly

Figure 5.2
(overleaf) Artist's reconstruction of a hunting scene (Dominic Andrews)

involved the use of boats, for example visiting the two islands, and while we have yet to find any examples of these, a wooden paddle was discovered by Clark. Elsewhere, people may have cut routes through the dense reed beds in order to travel through the wetlands, and paths and trails may have been laid through the surrounding forest.

Most of our evidence for hunting in this landscape comes from the bones of the animals themselves, several of which show traces of the weapons that were used to injure and kill them. The bones recovered in the various excavations indicate that people were hunting a wide range of animals. Some of these species live in very different habitats so people would have had to visit other parts of the landscape in order to hunt them. Aurochs and deer, for example, are largely terrestrial and would have been hunted in the woodlands or, perhaps, at the edge of the lake when they came to drink. In contrast, beavers are a wetland animal and may have been hunted in the lake itself.

People would also have gone out into the surrounding area to collect different species of plants and other raw materials that could be used for food or for the manufacture of artefacts. Some of the antlers that have been found at Star Carr had been shed naturally by the deer; these must have been collected by people in the surrounding landscape and brought back to site. Given the number of objects made from antler, this naturally shed material would have been an important resource and may have been kept until it was needed.

It is also clear that people travelled considerable distances to get the best-quality flint. This was obtained from the glacial deposits (known as till) on the coast, the nearest source being about 20km away. As there are no navigable water-courses leading directly to the coast from the lake, people would have had to make this journey on foot through the birch woodlands. This would have been a considerable undertaking which required a very good understanding of the geography of the surrounding area.

While much of what we know about Star Carr comes from scatters of worked flint and the objects of bone and antler, life would have involved more than just making and using tools, hunting animals or collecting plants. We know from the scatters of burnt flint that people were building hearths or fires, where they would have prepared food, or sat round together as they ate, telling stories and exchanging news. We can imagine the sounds as people shouted greetings to one another, the excitement as hunters returned with their kill, the laughter as people told jokes, the rustling of branches and reeds in the wind and the water of the lake lapping at the shore. The air would have been thick with the smell of smoke and cooking food, the dampness of the swamp and the woodland undergrowth. This was a place that people experienced with their senses; it was a place that was familiar to them; it was their home.

Figure 5.3 *Artist's reconstruction of people living at Star Carr (Dominic Andrews)*

Glossary

6

Blade   A long, thin piece of stone produced by knapping. This can either be used directly as an implement for cutting or can be worked further to produce tools such as microliths.

Burin   A stone tool, often thought to have been used for bone and antler working. A burin is made by sharpening the end of a flake or blade to produce a small, pointed cutting edge. The small pieces of stone that are produced when making or resharpening the cutting edge are known as 'burin spalls'.

Core   A piece of stone that has been worked by knapping so that regularly shaped blades can be struck from it.

Debitage   The waste material produced by knapping.

Flake   A piece of stone that has been detached or broken off a larger piece of material through knapping. This is either discarded as waste, utilised in its current form (usually as an implement for cutting), or worked further to produce a formal tool such as a burin or scraper.

Flint   A fine- and regular-grained stone found in chalk, which was used extensively to produce tools during the Stone Age.

Holocene   The current geological epoch, which follows the end of the last Ice Age.

Knapping   A method of working stone by striking the material in order to break off smaller pieces. This is also known as chipping or flaking. The purpose of knapping is either to shape a piece of raw material into a particular form (as in the manufacture of axes of cores) or to remove smaller pieces which can then be used as they are or worked further to produce tools (such as microliths or burins).

Maglemosian   The term given to the early Mesolithic period in southern Scandinavia. The name comes from the site of Maglemose (Denmark), which was excavated by George Sarauw at the start of the 20th century.

Microlith   A small piece of worked stone that has been manufactured from a blade and hafted onto a piece of wood, bone, or antler to produce objects such as knives, saws or arrows. A microlith is made by notching and snapping a larger blade and then retouching the edges. Depending on the technique used, this can produce a distinctive piece of waste material known as a micro-burin.

Preboreal   A term used to describe the first few centuries after the end of the last Ice Age, when a relatively open landscape of grassland and scrub vegetation was replaced with more extensive woodland cover.

Preboreal oscillation   A short-lived period of colder climate lasting approximately 200 years that occurred shortly after the end of the last Ice Age.

Retouching   Modifying the edge of a piece of worked stone, either to make it sharper (for use as a cutting tool) or blunter (so that it can be held more easily).

Use wear-analysis   The study of the traces (both macroscopic and microscopic) left on stone tools by the materials they have been used to cut or scrape; this can help to identify the function of the tool.

Younger Dryas   The final cold phase at the end of the last Ice Age.

Acknowledgements

7

The research presented in this book has only been possible through the support of a large number of people and institutions.

We are extremely grateful to all the landowners who have given us access to their land over the years.

We are also indebted to the Vale of Pickering Research Trust which has provided continuous financial support and guidance since 1985. The current trustees are Richard Marriott (Chair), Adrian Green, Graham Harvey, Jim Innes, Martin Jones, Peter Rowley-Conwy, Martin Millett, Tim Schadla-Hall, Richard Senior and Dominic Tweddle.

We are very grateful to the following institutions for recent grants to work at Star Carr: Ancient Monument division of the former Department of the Environment, North Yorkshire County Council, British Academy, English Heritage, the Natural Environment Research Council, European Research Council (POSTGLACIAL), University of Manchester, University of York, University College London and the McDonald Institute Cambridge. We also thank the POSTGLACIAL advisory board members for all their guidance: Graeme Barker, Martin Bell, Berit Eriksen, Carl Heron, Edward Impey and Tim Schadla-Hall.

The research has been undertaken by a large number of specialists who have shown a keen interest in the excavations and who visited on many occasions: Bruce Albert, Enid Allison, Alex Bayliss, Edward Blinkhorn, Simon Blockley, Julie Borehan, Steve Boreham, Mike Buckley, Ian Candy, Matthew Collins, Oliver Craig, Ben Elliott, Simon Fitch, Charly French, Helen Goodchild, Ben Gourley, Allan Hall, Kirsty High, Jim Innes, Harry Kenward, Becky Knight, Pete Langdon, Aimée Little, Anthony Masinton,

Ian Matthews, Richard McPhail, Helen Moulden, Terry O'Connor, Adrian Palmer, Ian Panter, Kirsty Penkman, James Rackham, Harry Robson, Lisa-Marie Shillitoe, Maisie Taylor and Sarah Viner.

We are extremely grateful to all the many wonderful diggers over the years, especially Chris Evans who has been digging with us since the 1970s, as well as students who have supervised and taken roles as research assistants, in particular Edward Blinkhorn, Ben Elliott, Amy Gray Jones, Pat Hadley, Emily Hellewell, Becky Knight, Andy Needham, Ray Nilson, Nick Overton, Harry Robson and Hayley Saul.

We would also like to thank the following people for their continuing interest, help and support in the project: Richard Bradley, Tim Burkinshaw, Alec Dickson, David Duncan, Keith Emerick, Gail Falkingham, Jon Finch, Tracey Gibson, Amy Gray Jones, Jane Grenville, Paul Lane, Phillip Lane, Jonathan Last, Sally Marriott, Claire McNamara, Margaret Nieke, Dominic Powlesland, Francis Pryor, Neil Redfern, Julian Richards, Jackie Roberts, Johanna Senior, Barney Sloane, Linda Smith, Terry Suthers, Richard Toole and Thomas Yarrow.

Thanks go to the following people and institutions for permission to use their figures (copyright remains with them):

Chapter 1
Figure 1.3 Dr Allan Hall

Chapter 2
Figure 2.1 Dr Pamela Jane Smith and the Cambridge studio of Lettice Ramsey and Helen Muspratt
Figure 2.3 Professor Vince Gaffney
Figures 2.5 and 2.9 Professor Lars Larsson
Figure 2.6 Wessex Archaeology
Figure 2.11 Dominic Andrews
Figure 2.12 Archaeological Consultancy Services Ltd
Figure 2.13 Dr Clive Waddington
Figure 2.14 Svetlana Savchenko and Mikhail Zhilin (original drawing by Vladimir Tolmachev)
Figure 2.15 Cambridge Museum of Archaeology and Anthropology
Figure 2.16 E Sacre, Goldcliff Project
Figure 2.18 Aegis Archaeology Limited
Figure 2.19 Dr Richard Brunning and Somerset County Council Museum Service

Figure 2.20 Vedbækfundene, Rudersdal Museer, with the kind assistance of Anne Birgitte Gurlev (photographer Ole Tage Hartmann)

Chapter 3

Figure 3.1 Gunilla and Mike Austin

Figures 3.4 and 3.5 Scarborough Archaeological and Historical Society

Figures 3.6 and 3.7a–e Cambridge Museum of Archaeology and Anthropology

Chapter 5

Figures 5.1–5.3 Dominic Andrews

We would also like to thank Jessica Rippengal for providing the image of the aurochs skull in Figure 2.4, and Emma Bauzyte for drawing the timber platform in Figure 3.9. The image of Nicky Milner on p 103 was taken by Ian Martindale (www.allisterfreeman.co.uk/ianmartindale).

Finally, we are grateful for the advice and comments of Frances Mee, Martin Millett, Chris Scarre and Paul Stamper on various versions of this text. Special thanks are due to Catrina Appleby of the CBA for suggesting the idea of this book and for all her support and guidance in the publication process.

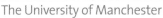

The authors

8

Nicky Milner

Nicky Milner is a Professor at the University of York. She did
a BA at the University of Nottingham (1992–95) and a PhD at
Cambridge (1995–98) and then went to the University of Newcastle
upon Tyne as a Sir James Knott Fellow, followed by a lecturing
position until 2004 when she moved to York.

She started digging in the Vale of Pickering with Dominic
Powlesland at the Anglo-Saxon settlement of West Heslerton in
1990; as well as working there for a number of years, she also
worked on a number of projects, both research and commercial,
in Britain as well as in France, Greece, Croatia, Ireland, Portugal,
Spain and Guernsey. In 1997 she joined the Vale of Pickering
Research Trust team working around Lake Flixton and in 2004
began to co-direct excavations at Star Carr with Barry Taylor
and Chantal Conneller. She has also co-directed fieldwork in
Ireland (with Peter Woodman) and Northumberland (with
Clive Waddington and Geoff Bailey). Her research focuses on
the Mesolithic period and she has a particular interest in both
wetland sites and coastal archaeology.

Barry Taylor

Barry Taylor is a post-doctoral research assistant at the University
of York. He did his BA and MA at the University of Durham (1993–
96 and 1998–2000) and his PhD at the University of Manchester
(2007–12).

Barry began working in the Vale of Pickering in 1991 as a volunteer on Dominic Powlesland's excavations at West Heslerton, and went on to work on the Mesolithic sites around Lake Flixton in 1995 when he was an undergraduate. Since then he has worked in commercial archaeology and for English Heritage but has maintained a close involvement with the work of the Vale of Pickering Research Trust. He has co-directed the excavations at Star Carr since 2004 and works with Nicky Milner on the late Palaeolithic and early Mesolithic site of Flixton Island. He also co-directs the excavations on the Mesolithic site of Flixton School House Farm on the southern shore of the lake (with Dr Amy Gray Jones) and has carried out extensive surveys of the lake and its environs. His research focuses on the reconstruction of ancient environments through the analysis of plant remains preserved in peat and lake sediments, the use of plants by Mesolithic hunter-gatherers, and theoretical approaches to the study of past landscapes.

Chantal Conneller

Chantal Conneller is senior lecturer at the University of Manchester. She did her BA and PhD at the University of Cambridge, worked at the Cambridge Archaeological Unit 1994–95 and 2000–01 and held a research fellowship at Queens' College Cambridge between 2001 and 2004. In 2005 she took up a post as lecturer at Bangor University before moving to Manchester.

Chantal has worked on the Mesolithic of the Vale of Pickering since 1995 when she started her PhD on the stone tools from the Seamer and Vale of Pickering Trust sites, and she has excavated with the Trust since 1997. She has worked on Mesolithic sites in the Pennines and directed excavations at the Upper Palaeolithic site of Rookery Farm, Cambridgeshire. Since 2004, she has co-directed excavations at Star Carr with Nicky Milner and Barry Taylor. She also currently co-directs the Quaternary Archaeology of Jersey project and excavations at the Upper Palaeolithic site of Ffynnon Beuno, Denbighshire. Her research focuses on the Upper Palaeolithic and Mesolithic periods and she has a special interest in stone tool technology, material culture studies and human perceptions of animals.

Tim Schadla-Hall

Tim Schadla-Hall is a Reader in Public Archaeology at the Institute of Archaeology, University College London. He did his BA and MA at Cambridge (1971–73 and 1974) and has held numerous posts including Wessex Archaeological Committee Field Survey Officer; Senior Keeper of Archaeology for Hampshire Museums Service; Principal Keeper for Hull Museums; and Director of Museums, Arts and Records at Leicestershire County Council (1992–98).

Tim grew up working on excavations in East Yorkshire and Dorset and has worked extensively on the Mesolithic archaeology of the eastern Vale of Pickering, first as director of the Seamer Carr project (1975–85) and then as the fieldwork director for the Vale of Pickering Research Trust (1985 to the present). He directed the 1985 excavations at Star Carr, and co-directed the excavations at the site with Nicky Milner, Barry Taylor and Chantal Conneller in 2004–05. He is currently working on a major synthesis of the Mesolithic archaeology and environments of Lake Flixton (with Dr Paul Lane). He has recently carried out research on the landscape history of Boynton Hall in East Yorkshire (with Dr Adrian Green).

Bibliography

9

Albrethsen, S E & Brinch Petersen, E, 1976 Excavation of a Mesolithic cemetery at Vedbaek, Denmark, *Acta Archaeologica* **47**, 1–28

Allen, M J & Gardiner, J, 2002 A sense of time. Cultural markers in the Mesolithic of southern England, in D Bruno & M Wilson (eds) *Inscribed landscapes; marking and making place.* Honolulu: University of Hawaii Press, 139–53

Andersen, S H, 1987 Tybrind Vig: A submerged Ertebølle settlement in Denmark, in J M Coles & A J Lawson (eds) *European wetlands in prehistory.* Oxford: Clarendon Press, 253–79

Andersen, S H, 1995 Coastal adaptation and marine exploitation in late Mesolithic Denmark,with special emphasis on the Limfjord region, in A Fischer (ed) *Man and sea in the Mesolithic.* Oxford: Oxbow, 41–66

Andrefsky, W, 1998 *Lithics, macroscopic approaches to analysis.* Cambridge: Cambridge University Press

Andresen, J, Byrd, B, Elson, M, McGuire, R, Mendoza, R, Staski, E & White, P, 1981 The deer hunters: Star Carr reconsidered, *World Archaeology* **13**:1, 31–46

Bailey, G & Spikins, P, 2008 *Mesolithic Europe.* Cambridge: Cambridge University Press

Bell, M, 2007 *Prehistoric Coastal Communities: the Mesolithic in western Britain,* CBA Res Rep **149**. York: Council for British Archaeology

Bell, M & Walker, M J C, 2005 *Late quaternary environmental change. Physical and human perspectives.* Harlow: Pearson Education Limited

Blankholm, H P, 2008 Southern Scandinavia, in Bailey & Spikins (eds) 2008, 107–31

Boreham, S, Conneller, C, Milner, N, Taylor, B, Needham, A, Boreham, J & Rolfe, C J, 2011 Geochemical indicators of preservation status and site deterioration at Star Carr, *J Archaeol Sci* **38**:10, 2833–57

Brinch Petersen, P & Meiklejohn, C, 2003 Three cremations and a funeral: Aspects of burial practice in Mesolithic Vedbaek, *in* S B McCartan, R Schulting, G Warren & P Woodman (eds) *Mesolithic Horizons. Papers presented at the sixth international conference on the Mesolithic in Europe, Belfast 2005.* Oxford: Oxbow, 465–72

Brunning, R & Firth, H, 2009. An early Mesolithic cemetery at Greylake, Somerset, UK, *PAST* **69**, 6–8

Burrow, S, 2003 *Catalogue of the Mesolithic and Neolithic collections at the National Museums and Galleries of Wales*. Cardiff: National Museums & Galleries of Wales

Carter, R J, 1998 Reassessment of seasonality at the early Mesolithic site of Star Carr, Yorkshire, based on radiographs of mandibular tooth development in red deer (*Cervus elaphus*), *J Archaeol Sci* **25**:9, 851–6

Caulfield, S, 1978 Star Carr – an alternative view, *Irish Archaeol Research Forum* **5**, 15–22

Chaix, L, Bridault, A & Picavetc, R, 1997 A tamed Brown Bear (*Ursus arctos L.*) of the late Mesolithic from La Grande-Rivoire (Isère, France)?, *J Archaeol Sci* **24**:12, 1067–74

Chatterton, R, 2003 Star Carr reanalysed, in J Moore & L Bevan (eds) *Peopling the Mesolithic in a northern environment*, BAR Internat Series **1157**. Oxford: Archaeopress, 69–80

Clark, J G D, 1932 *The Mesolithic age in Britain*. Cambridge: Cambridge University Press

Clark, J G D, 1936 *The Mesolithic settlement of northern Europe. A study of the food-gathering peoples of northern Europe during the early post-glacial period.* Cambridge: Cambridge University Press

Clark, J G D, 1954 *Excavations at Star Carr*. Cambridge: Cambridge University Press

Clark, J G D, 1972 *Star Carr: a case study in bioarchaeology*. Reading (Massachusetts): Addison-Wesley Publishing Co

Clarke, D, 1978 *Mesolithic Europe: the economic basis*. London: Duckworth

Cloutman, E, 1988 Palaeoenvironments in the Vale of Pickering, Part 2: environmental history at Seamer Carr, *Proc Prehist Soc* **54**, 21–36

Cloutman, E & Smith, A G, 1988 Palaeoenvironments in the Vale of Pickering, Part 3: environmental history at Star Carr, *Proc Prehist Soc* **54**, 37–58

Collins, T & Coyne, F, 2003 Fire and water … Early Mesolithic cremations at Hermitage, Co. Limerick, *Archaeol Ireland* **64** (Summer), 24–7

Conneller, C, 2003 Star Carr recontextualised, in J Moore & L Bevan (eds) *Peopling the Mesolithic in a northern environment*, BAR Internat Series **1157**. Oxford: Archaeopress, 81–6

Conneller, C, 2004 Becoming deer: corporeal transformations at Star Carr, *Archaeol Dialogues* **11**, 37–56

Conneller, C, 2006 Death, in Conneller & Warren (eds) 2006, 139–64

Conneller, C, 2007 Inhabiting new landscapes: Settlement and mobility in Britain after the last glacial maximum, *Oxford J Archaeol* **26**:3, 215–37

Conneller, C & Schadla-Hall, R T, 2003 Beyond Star Carr: the Vale of Pickering in the tenth millennium BP, *Proc Prehist Soc* **69**, 85–105

Conneller, C & Warren, W (eds), 2006 *Mesolithic Britain and Ireland. New Approaches*. Stroud: Tempus

Conneller, C, Milner, N, Schadla-Hall, R T & Taylor, B 2009a Star Carr in the new millennium, in N Finlay, S McCartan, N Milner & C Wickham-Jones (eds) *From Bann flakes to Bushmills. Papers in honour of Professor Peter Woodman*, *Prehist Soc Research Paper* **1**. Oxford: Oxbow, 78–88

Conneller, C, Milner, N, Schadla-Hall, R T & Taylor, B, 2009b The temporality of the Mesolithic landscape: new work at Star Carr, in P Crombé, M Van Strydonck, J Sergant, M Boudin & M Bats (eds) *Chronology and evolution within the Mesolithic of north-west Europe. Proceedings of international meeting, Brussels.* Newcastle upon Tyne: Cambridge Scholars Publishing, 77–94

Conneller, C, Milner, N & Taylor, B, 2010 New finds at Star Carr, *Brit Academy Review* **16**

Conneller, C, Milner, N, Taylor, B & Taylor, M, 2012 Substantial settlement in the European early Mesolithic: new research at Star Carr, *Antiquity* **86**:334, 1004–20

Cummins, G, 2000 Fire! Accidental or strategic use of fire in the early Mesolithic of the eastern Vale of Pickering, in R Young (ed) *Mesolithic lifeways. Current research from Britain and Ireland,* Leicester Archaeology Monographs **7**. Leicester: University of Leicester, 75–86

Cunliffe, B, 1994 *The Oxford Illustrated History of Prehistoric Europe*. Oxford: Oxford University Press

Dark, P, 1998 Palaeoecological investigations, in Mellars & Dark 1998

Dark, P, 2004 Plant remains as evidence for seasonality of site use in the Mesolithic period, *Environmental Archaeol* **9**, 39–45

Dark, P, Higham, T F G, Jacobi, R & Lord, T, 2006 New radiocarbon accelerator dates on artefacts from the early Mesolithic site of Star Carr, North Yorkshire, *Archaeometry* **48**:1, 185–200

Darvill, T, 2010 *Prehistoric Britain* (2nd edition). London: Routledge

Dumont, J V, 1988 *A microwear analysis of selected artifact types from the Mesolithic sites of Star Carr and Mount Sandel*. BAR Brit Series **187**. Oxford: British Archaeological Reports

Elliot, B J & Milner, N, 2010 Making a point. A critical review of the barbed point manufacturing process practised at Star Carr, *Proc Prehist Soc* **76**, 75–94

Ellis, C, Allen, J, Gardiner, J, Harding, P, Ingrem, C, Powell, A & Scaife, R, 2003 An early Mesolithic seasonal hunting site in the Kennet Valley, southern England, *Proc Prehist Soc* **69**, 107–36

Friis-Hansen, J, 1990 Mesolithic cutting arrows: functional analysis of arrows used in the hunting of large game, *Antiquity* **64**:244, 494–504

Gaffney, V, Fitch, S, & Smith, D, 2009 *Europe's lost world. The rediscovery of Doggerland,* CBA Res Rep **160**. York: Council for British Archaeology

Garcia-Moncó, C, 2009 Dogs and people, an arising relationship: *Canis familiaris* amongst hunter-gatherer societies in the Iberian Peninsula, in S McCartan, R Schulting, G Warren & P Woodman (eds) *Mesolithic Horizons: Papers presented at the Seventh International Conference on the Mesolithic in Europe, Belfast 2005*. Oxford: Oxbow, 675–82

Godwin, H, 1975 *History of the British flora. A factual basis for phytogeography* (2nd edition). Cambridge: Cambridge University Press

Godwin, H & Godwin, M E, 1933 British Maglemose harpoon sites, *Antiquity* **7**:25, 39–48

Grosman, L, Munro, N D & Belfer-Cohen, A, 2008 A 12,000 year old shaman burial from the southern Levant (Israel), *Proc National Academy Sci* **105**:46, 17665–9

Hardy, K, Birch, S & Shiel, R, 2009 Bevel-ended bone tools from Scottish Mesolithic sites, in S McCartan, R Schulting, G Warren & P Woodman (eds) *Mesolithic Horizons: Papers presented at the Seventh International Conference on the Mesolithic in Europe, Belfast 2005*. Oxford: Oxbow, 766–71

Holst, D, 2010 Hazelnut ecologies of early Holocene hunter-gatherers: a case study from Duvensee, Northern Germany, *J Archaeol Sci* **37**:11, 2871–80

Hunter, J & Ralston, I (eds), 2009 *The archaeology of Britain: An introduction from earliest times to the twenty-first century* (2nd edition). London: Routledge

Jacobi, R, 1978 Northern England in the eighth millennium bc: An essay, in P Mellars (ed) *The early post-glacial in Europe. An ecological perspective.* London: Duckworth, 295–332

Jensen, J, 1986 Unretouched blades in the late Mesolithic of southern Scandinavia. A functional study, *Oxford J Archaeol* **5**:1, 19–33

Jordan, P, 2003 Peopling the Mesolithic: insights from ethnographies of landscape and material culture, in L Bevan & J Moore (eds) *Peopling the Mesolithic in a northern Environment.* BAR Internat Series **1157**. Oxford: Archaeopress, 27–34

Kannegaard Nielson, E & Brinch Petersen, E, 1993 Burials, people and dogs, in S Hvass & B Storgaard (eds) *Digging into the past. 25 years of Archaeology in Denmark.* Aarhus Universitetsforlag, 76–81

Larsson, L, 1984 The Skateholm project: a late Mesolithic settlement and cemetery complex at a southern Swedish bay, *Meddelanden från Lunds Universitets Historiska Museum 1983–84*, 5–46

Larsson, L, 1989 Late Mesolithic settlements and cemeteries at Skateholm, southern Sweden, in C Bonsall (ed) *The Mesolithic in Europe. Papers presented at the third international symposium, Edinburgh 1985.* Edinburgh: John Donald, 367–78

Larsson, L, 1990 Dogs in fraction – symbols in action, in P Vermeersch & P van Peer (eds) *Contributions to the Mesolithic in Europe.* Leuven: Leuven University Press, 153–60

Larsson, L & Sjöström, S, 2010 Mesolithic research in the bog Rönneholms mosse, southern Sweden, *Mesolithic Miscellany* **21**:1, 2–9

Law, C, 1998 The uses and fire-ecology of reedswamp vegetation, in Mellars & Dark 1998, 197–207

Legge, A & Rowley-Conwy, P, 1988 *Star Carr revisited: a re-analysis of the large mammals.* London: Centre for Extra-Mural Studies

Lowe, J J & Walker, M J C, 1997 *Reconstructing Quaternary environments* (2nd edition). Harlow: Longman

McQuade, M & O'Donnell, L, 2007 Late Mesolithic fish traps from the Liffey estuary, Dublin, Ireland, *Antiquity* **81**:313, 569–84

Meiklejon, C, Merrett, D C, Nolan, R W, Richards, M P & Mellars, P M, 2005 Spatial relationships, dating and taphonomy of the human bone from the Mesolithic site of Cnoc Coig, Oronsay, Argyll, Scotland, *Proc Prehist Soc* **71**, 85–105

Mellars, P, 1987 *Excavations on Oronsay: prehistoric human ecology on a small island.* Edinburgh: Edinburgh University Press

Mellars, P & Dark, P, 1998 *Star Carr in context: new archaeological and palaeoecological investigations at the early Mesolithic site of Star Carr, North Yorkshire.* Cambridge: McDonald Institute for Archaeological Research

Milner, N, 1999 Pitfalls and problems in analysing and interpreting the seasonality of faunal remains, in N Milner, D Q Fuller, & M Baxter (eds) Contending with bones, *Archaeol Review from Cambridge* **16**, 51–67

Milner, N, 2007 Fading Star, *British Archaeology* **96**, 10–14

Milner, N & Woodman, P C, 2005 Looking into the Canon's mouth: Mesolithic studies in the 21st Century, in N Milner & P C Woodman (eds) *Mesolithic studies at the beginning of the 21st century.* Oxford: Oxbow, 1–13

Milner, N, Conneller, C, Elliott, B, Koon, H, Panter, I, Penkman, K, Taylor, B & Taylor, M, 2011 From riches to rags: organic deterioration at Star Carr, *J Archaeol Sci* **38**:10, 2818–32

Milner, N, Lane, P, Taylor, B, Conneller, C & Schadla-Hall, T, 2011 Star Carr in a
post-glacial lakescape: 60 years of research, *J Wetland Archaeol* **11**, 1–19

Mithen, S, 2003 *After the Ice. A global human history.* London: Pheonix

Mithen, S, 2010 *To the Islands: An Archaeologist's Relentless Quest to Find the
Prehistoric Hunter-Gatherers of the Hebrides.* Isle of Lewis: Two Ravens Press

Mithen, S, Finlay N, Carruthers, W, Carter, S & Ashmore, P, 2001 Plant use in the
Mesolithic: evidence from Staosnaig, Isle of Colonsay, Scotland, *J Archaeol Sci*
28:3, 223–4

Moore, J, 1950 Mesolithic sites in the neighbourhood of Flixton, north-east
Yorkshire, *Proc Prehist Soc* **16**, 101–08

Moore, J, 1951 *Lake Flixton: a late-glacial structure.* Scarborough: Scarborough &
District Archaeological Society

Moore, J, 1954 Excavations at Flixton site 2, in Clark 1954, 192–4

Murray, H K, Murray, J C & Shannon, M F, 2009 *A tale of the unknown unknowns:
a Mesolithic pit alignment and a Neolithic timber hall at Warren Field, Crathes,
Aberdeenshire.* Oxford: Oxbow

Nilsson Stutz, L, 2003 *Embodied rituals & ritualized bodies: tracing ritual practices in
late Mesolithic burials.* Lund: Wallin & Dahlholm

Noe-Nygaard, N, 1974 Mesolithic hunting in Denmark illustrated by bone injuries
caused by human weapons, *J Archaeol Sci* **1**:3, 217–48

Out, W, 2009 *Sowing the seed? Human impact and plant subsistence in Dutch wetlands
during the late Mesolithic and early and middle Neolithic (5500–3400 cal BC).*
Leiden: Leiden University Press

Pettitt, P & White, M, 2012 *The British Palaeolithic. Hominin societies at the edge of
the Pleistocene world.* Oxford: Routledge

Pollard, J, 2000 Ancestral places in the Mesolithic landscape, in C Conneller
(ed) New approaches to the Palaeolithic and Mesolithic, *Archaeol Review from
Cambridge* **17**:1, 123–38

Porr, M & Alt, K W, 2006 The Burial of Bad Dürrenberg, central Germany:
osteopathology and osteoarchaeology of a late Mesolithic shaman's grave,
Internat J Osteoarchaeol **16**:5, 395–406

Rowley-Conwy, P, 1996 Why didn't Westropp's 'Mesolithic' catch on in 1872?
Antiquity **70**:270, 940–4

Rowley-Conwy, P, 2010 From Great Bog to Sedge Fen: a note on Grahame Clark's
interpretation of Star Carr in its landscape context, in A Marciniak & J Coles
(eds) *Grahame Clark and his Legacy.* Newcastle upon Tyne: Cambridge Scholars,
68–84

Rydin, H & Jeglum, J, 2006 *The biology of peatlands.* Oxford: Oxford University
Press

Saville, A (ed), 2004 *Mesolithic Scotland and its Neighbours. The early Holocene
prehistory of Scotland, its British and Irish context, and some Northern European
perspectives.* Edinburgh: Society of Antiquaries of Scotland

Schulting, R J, 2005 '...pursuing a rabbit in Burrington Combe'. New research on
the early Mesolithic burial cave of Aveline's Hole, *Proc University of Bristol
Spelaeological Soc* **23**, 171–265

Simmons, I G, 2001 *An Environmental History of Great Britain: from 10,000 Years Ago
to the Present.* Edinburgh: Edinburgh University Press

Smith, C, 1992 *Stone Age Hunters of the British Isles.* London: Routledge

Smith, P, 1997 Grahame Clark's new archaeology: the Fenland Research
Committee and Cambridge prehistory in the 1930s, *Antiquity* **71**:271, 11–30

Taylor, B, 2007 Recent excavations at Star Carr, North Yorkshire, *Mesolithic Miscellany* **18**:2, 12–16

Taylor, B, 2011 Early Mesolithic activity in the wetlands of the Lake Flixton basin, *J Wetland Archaeol* **11**, 63–84

Taylor, B, 2013 The history of environmental archaeology at Star Carr, in C Smith (ed) *Encyclopedia of Global Archaeology*. New York: Springer

Taylor, B & Gray Jones, A, 2009 Definitely a pit, possibly a house? Recent excavations at Flixton School House Farm in the Vale of Pickering, *Mesolithic Miscellany* **20**:2, 21–6

Taylor, B, Conneller, C & Milner, N, 2010. Little house by the shore, *British Archaeology* **115**

Tolan-Smith, C, 2008 Mesolithic Britain, in Bailey & Spikins (eds) 2008, 132–57

Waddington, C (ed), 2007 *Mesolithic settlement in the North Sea basin. A case study from Howick, north-east England*. Oxford: Oxbow

Warren, G, 2005 *Mesolithic Lives in Scotland*. Stroud: Tempus

Weninger, B, Schulting, R, Bradtmöller, M, Clare, L, Collard, M, Edinborough, K, Hilpert, J, Jöris, O, Niekus, M, Rohling, E J & Wagner, B, 2008 The catastrophic final flooding of Doggerland by the Storegga Slide tsunami, *Documenta Praehistorica* **XXXV**, 1–24

Wickham-Jones, C, 1990 *Rhum, Mesolithic and later sites at Kinloch, excavations 1984–1986*, Soc of Antiq Scotland Monogr **7**. Edinburgh: Society of Antiquaries of Scotland

Yalden, D W, 1999 *The history of British mammals*. London: T & A D Poyser

Zvelebil, M, 1994 Plant use in the Mesolithic and its role in the transition to farming, *Proc Prehist Soc* **60**, 35–74